I0472367

# Port Hope Ontario Book 3 in Colour Photos, Saving Our History One Photo at a Time

Photography
by Barbara Raué
©2019

Series Name: Cruising Ontario

Book 232: Port Hope Book 3

Cover photo: 345 Lakeshore Road, Page 27

# Table of Contents

Port Hope is located in Southern Ontario about 109 kilometers (68 miles) east of Toronto and about 159 kilometers (99 miles) west of Kingston. It is located at the mouth of the Ganaraska River on the north shore of Lake Ontario, in the west end of Northumberland County. Port Hope's nearest urban neighbor (25 kilometers to the west) is the City of Oshawa.

Before Canada became a nation in 1867, Port Hope was already a boomtown. Its main streets were thronged with horse-drawn carriages and farmers' wagons, its plank sidewalks crowded with shoppers and merchandise. Wood-burning locomotives pulled heavily loaded trains through town on their way to a harbor filled with schooners and steamships. Solid brick commercial blocks and houses lined the streets.

The town grew rapidly from four families of English descent who arrived by boat in 1793 and settled at the river mouth. The first European settlers came from the new United States. They had chosen to follow the British crown after the American Revolution. So had Elias Smith, a Montreal merchant who, with two partners, Jonathan and Abraham Walton, financed their arrival. In return for settling forty families on the land and building a sawmill and flourmill to serve them, the partners received a grant of land roughly the size of modern urban Port Hope.

More families arrived including blacksmiths, carpenters, bricklayers, and merchants. The mills drew farmers from fifty and sixty kilometers away. Grain that could not be milled was bought by distilleries — there were eventually five along the river — that produced a famous Port Hope whisky. Its most rapid growth began when railways revolutionized travel in what is now Ontario.

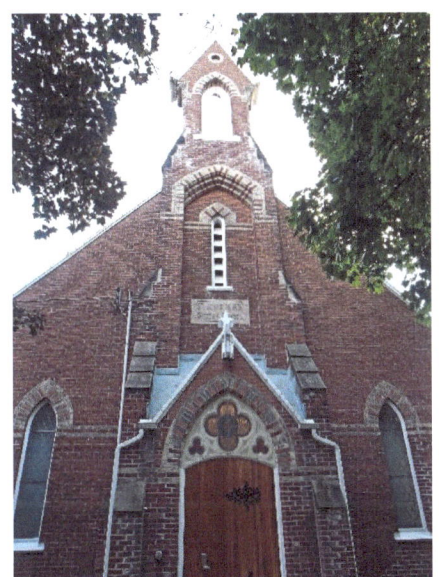
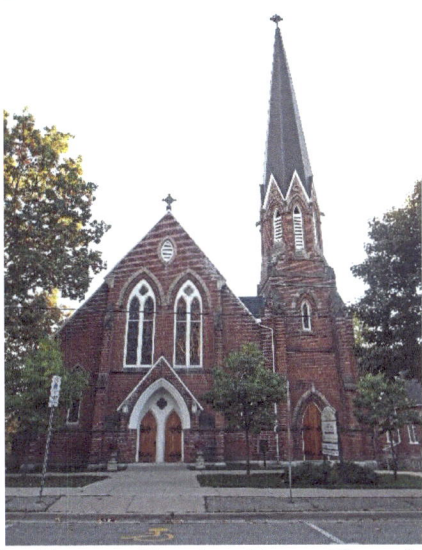

33 Pine Street North - St. John the Evangelist Anglican Church and Sunday School

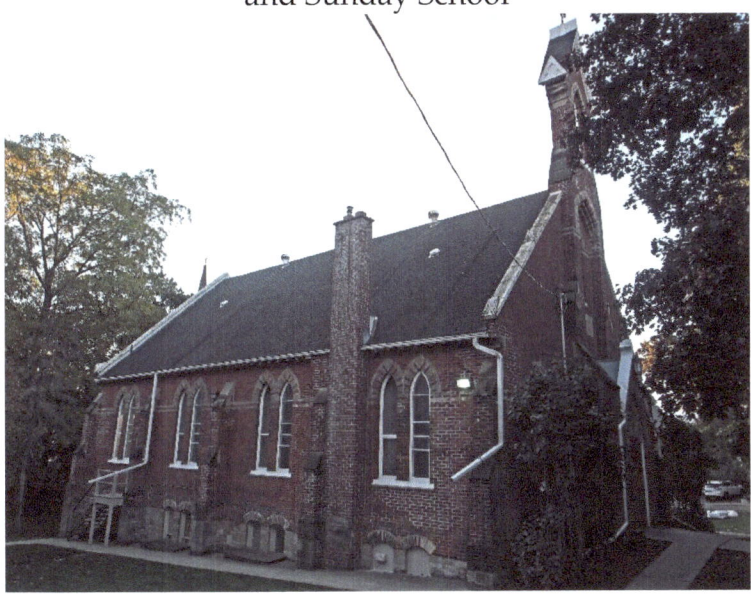

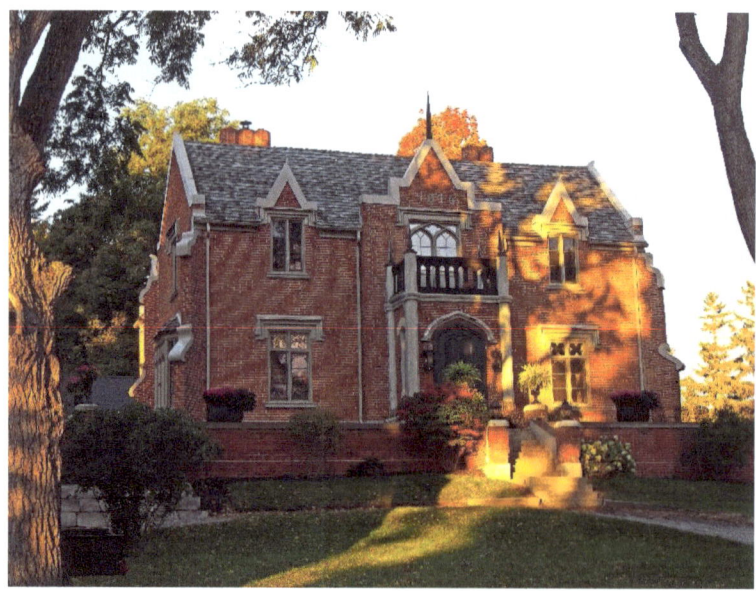

44 Pine Street North – c. 1846 - The two-storey brick house in the Tudor Manor style, Pinehurst, has a steeply pitched gable roof, two chimneys, decorative buttresses, stepped gables with thickly molded windows, and enclosed front porch. on the ground floor there are double casement sash windows with gothic tracery and a quatrefoil pattern in the top two panes. On the frontispiece above the brick porch is a Gothic arched double casement sash window. The brick porch is reinforced at the corners by attached pillars.

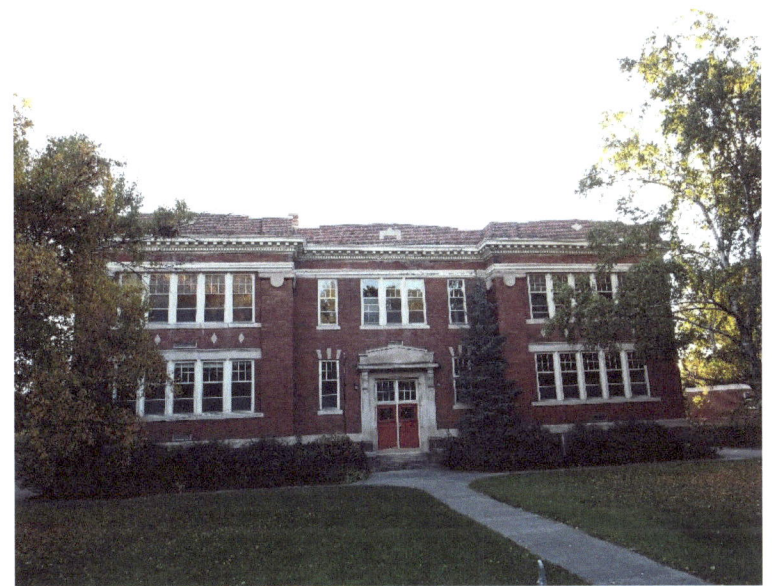

Pine Street North – School

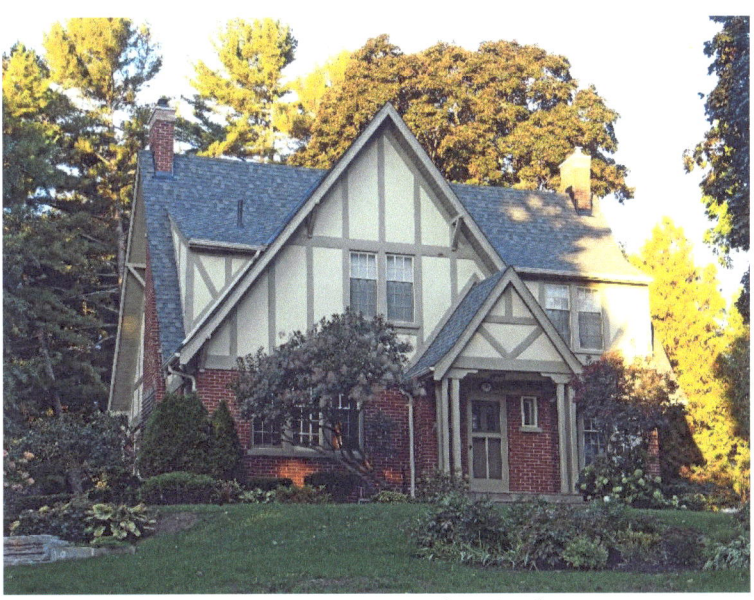

36 Pine Street North - Tudor

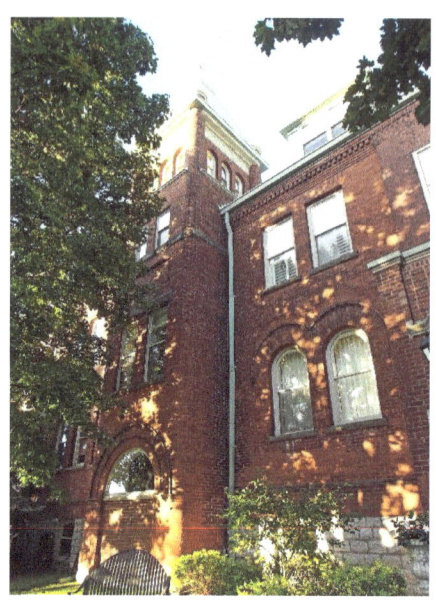

72 Pine Street North – The Pines of Port Hope – four-storey tower

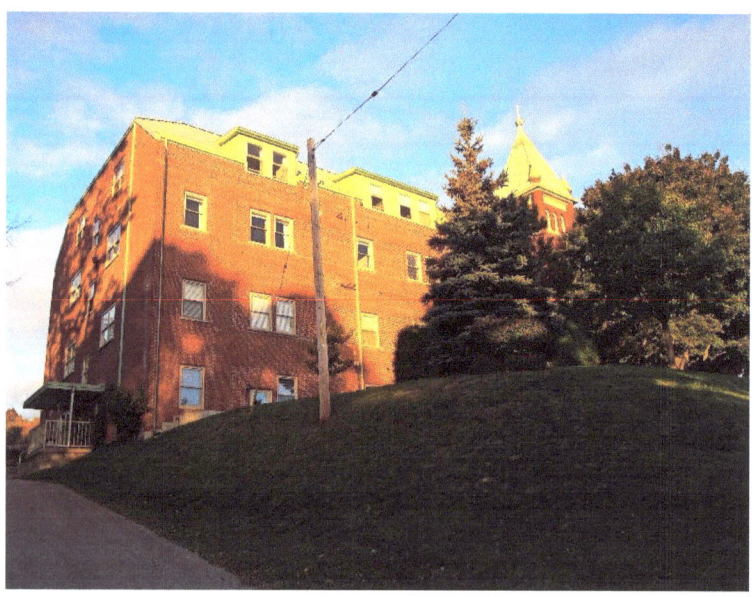

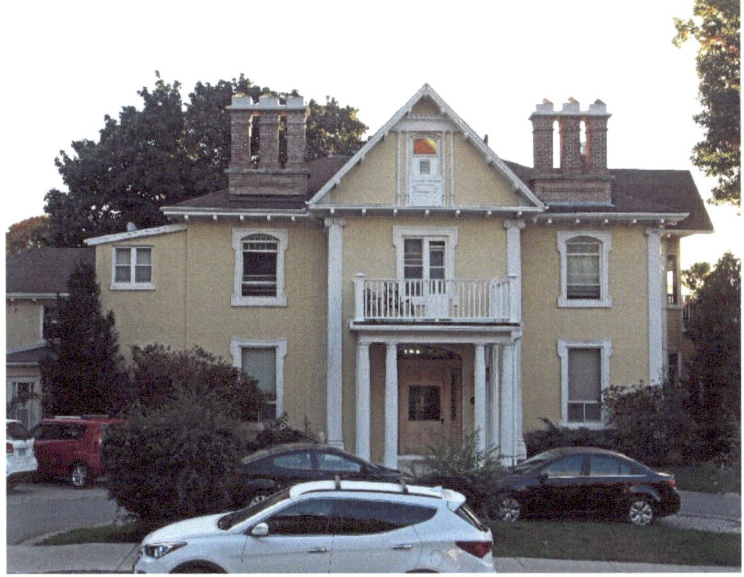

71 Pine Street North – c. 1855 - two-storey painted-brick structure with a hip roof – Vernacular in style. The chimneys are triple-flue design with projecting sill and panelled base. In line with the windows below, these appear to "float" over the windows. Each corner of the facade has Ionic pilasters that stretch the full height of the house. Portico over the front door has six turned Doric posts and two pilasters.

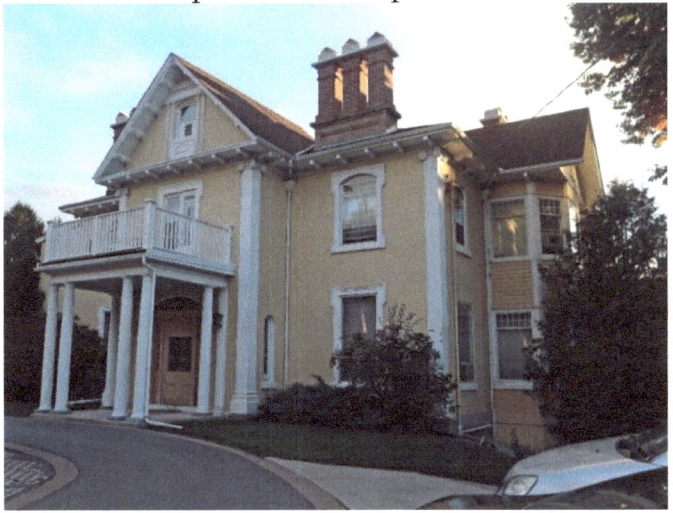

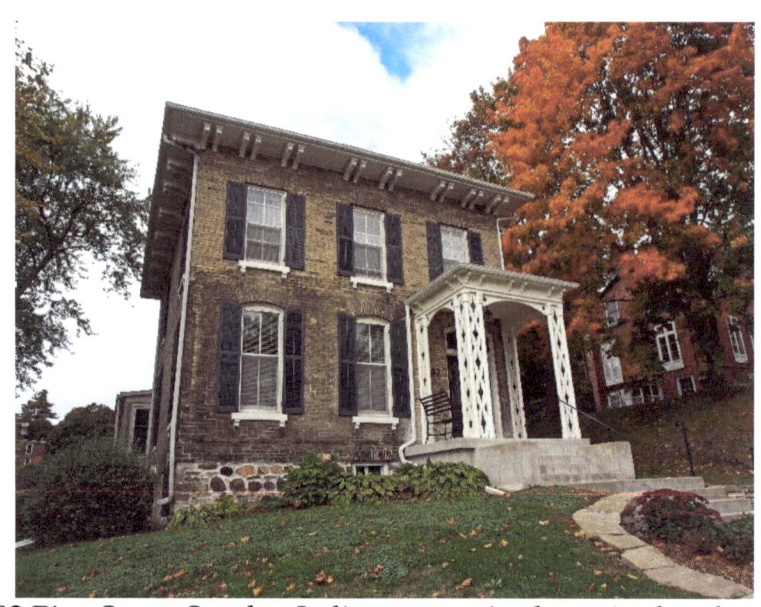

82 Pine Street South – Italianate – paired cornice brackets, rubble stone basement

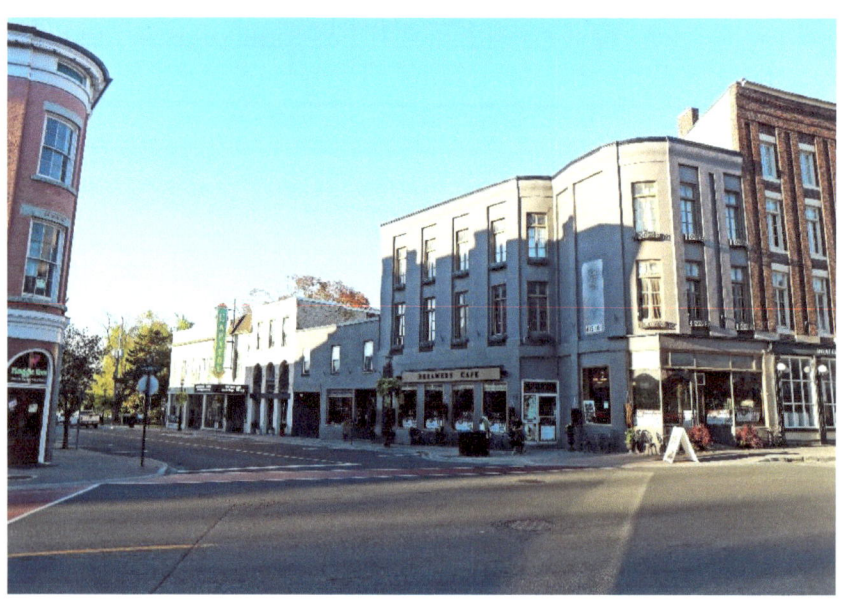

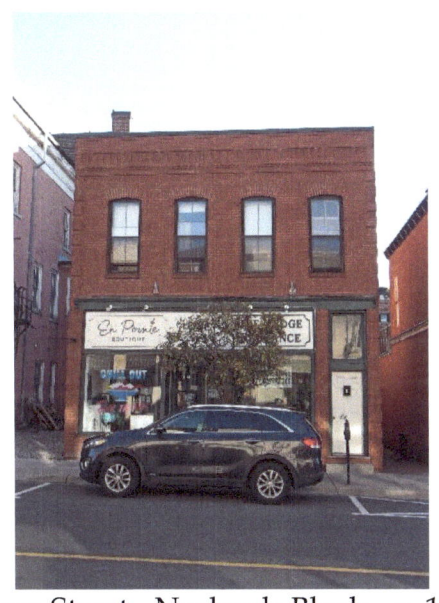

7-11 Queen Street - Neelands Block – c. 1876 - two storey L-shaped brick building - Dr. Thomas Neelands is thought to have arranged for the construction of this two-unit commercial block in 1876. Dr. Neelands (1842-1906) was born in Brampton in 1842 and studied Dentistry at the Royal College of Dental Surgeons in Toronto. He established a dental office in Port Hope in 1863. After this was built, he occupied the top floor of the Neelands Block and rented the street level north and south commercial areas.

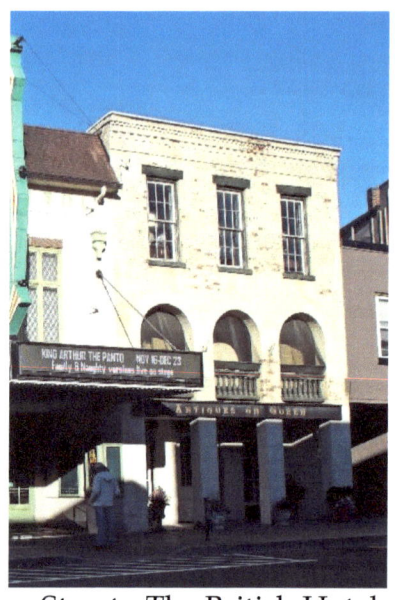

10-12 Queen Street - The British Hotel – c. 1845 - three-storey brick building - The front elevation of the building is three bays wide with an open arcade two storeys high. Within the arcade there is a porch at the second-floor level.

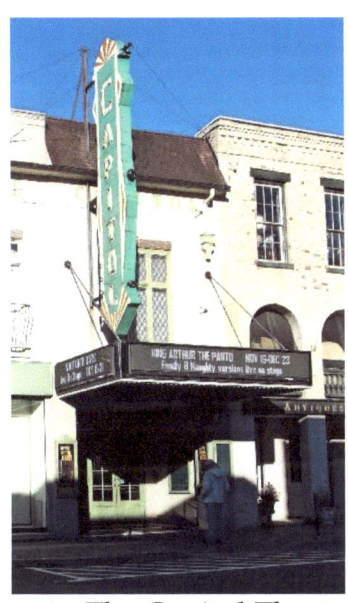

14 Queen Street - The Capitol Theatre – c. 1930 - The Capitol Theatre occupies sixteen feet of frontage on Queen Street. This section contains a hall lobby and expands in the rear to a 500-seat theatre. Throughout the theatre adopts an atmospheric theme, namely the courtyard of a medieval Norman castle. The castle theme is shown in diamond-paned windows, stucco finish (which bears the word "CAPITOL" along the cornice. The original marquee (since removed) was rectangular, and has been likened to a drawbridge.

The Capitol Theatre in Port Hope was designed and construction supervised by architect, Murray Brown for Famous Players. Brown was a former President of the Ontario Association of Architects. He had previously designed the theatres in Halifax and Saskatoon.

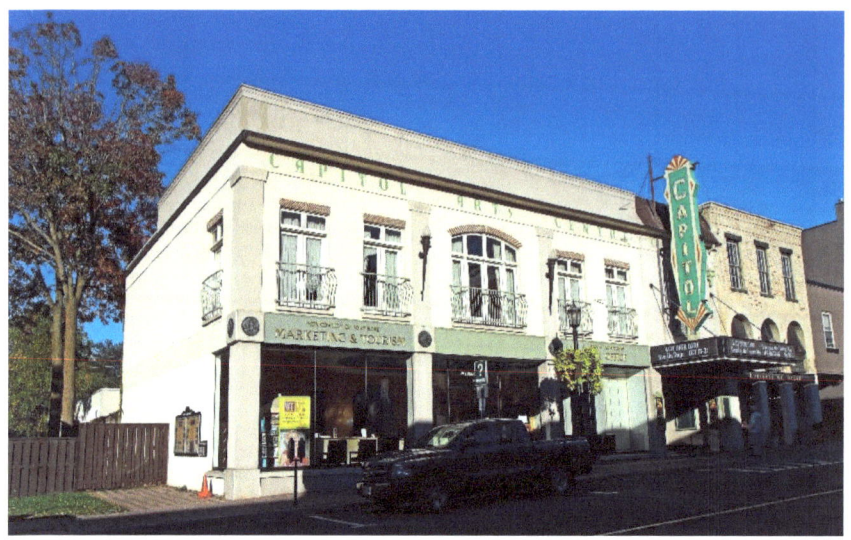

18-22 Queen Street – Stevenson Block – c. 1877 - This two-storey brick building was constructed with three storefronts on the ground floor and apartments above. The simple brick cornice, the circular second storey window heads and the recessed Victorian shop fronts combine to form a well-proportioned facade.

William Stevenson built this block in two stages. The first section was constructed in 1877. In 1879, the second section was constructed.

William G. Stevenson was born in Ireland in 1833. He appears in Port Hope business directories by 1871 as a tailor residing on William Street. When he had this commercial block built, his clothing store was located in the first section.

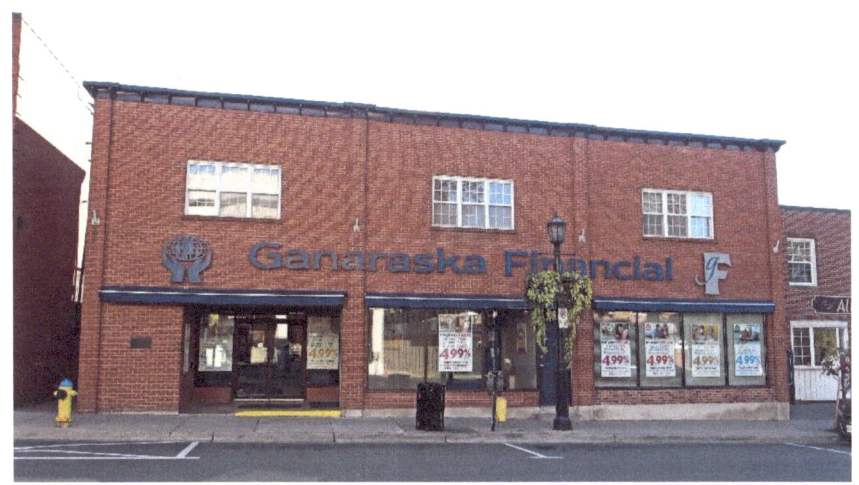

17 Queen Street

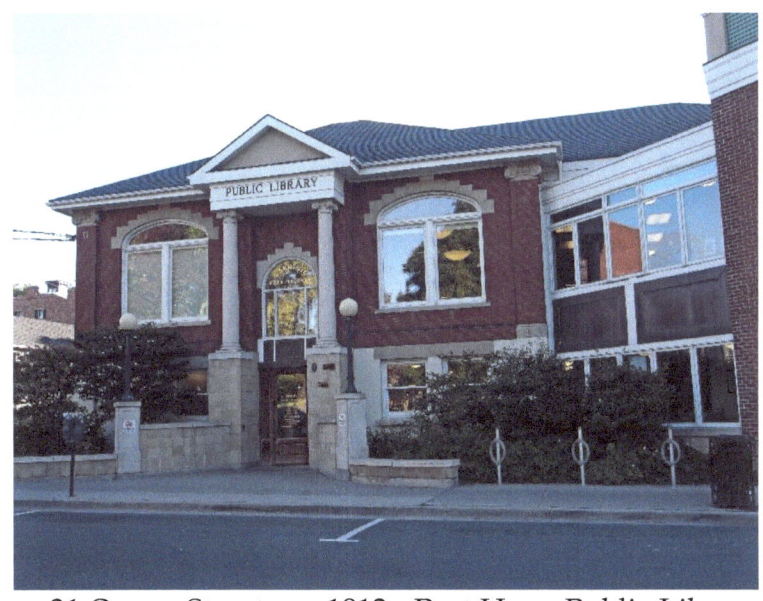

31 Queen Street – c. 1912 - Port Hope Public Library -

The original 1912 Carnegie Library, designed by Walter Mahoney, is a simple centre hall plan with the main floor on the second level containing the adult library and the lower level containing the children's library and the boiler room.

The architectural style is Greek Revival, a style which most Carnegie Libraries embraced due to its association with democracy and intellectual pursuits. The Port Hope Library had a large Portico entrance with a broad set of steps leading to the front door. The Portico was graced with large precast columns with Ionic capitals. The columns support a simple frieze and pediment made of wood and unadorned. The columns were supported by a masonry base flaring to accommodate a wide curved stair. The front door was a glazed wood door with a half round glass transom with an exaggerated precast lintel. The corners of the front facade had brick pilasters terminated in Ionic capitals matching the entrance columns. Port Hope's Carnegie Library underwent major renovations and expansion in 2002.

Between 1903 and 1924, over one hundred public libraries were constructed in Ontario as a result of grants from Andrew Carnegie (1835-1919), the Scottish born American industrialist and philanthropist, under the auspices of the Carnegie Corporation. The grant covered the cost of construction of a building with the only restriction being the library would be open to the public free of charge. Preference was given to small rather than large communities, and the amount of the grant was related to the size of the population.

Most of the original Carnegie libraries have been renovated or modified for alternate use. Of the sixty-six libraries designated as heritage properties, the majority are Carnegie Libraries.

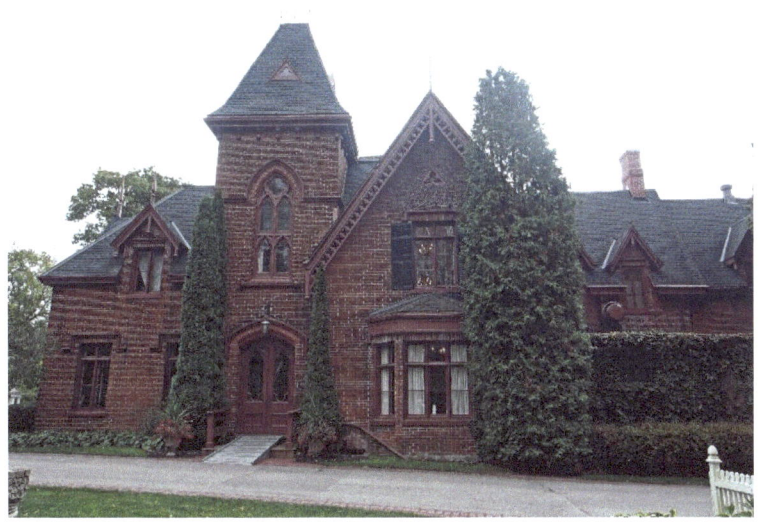

82 Victoria Street South - Arthur Trefusis Heneage Williams House (Penryn Park) – c. 1859 - Penryn Park is an excellent example of the Cottage Gothic house. It includes details such as bargeboard trim truer to the medieval pattern in their cusped and carved form than the lacy interpretation common to other buildings of the period. The house has hood moulds to openings and a Chinese pagoda roof over a rear second-storey window and a tower at the entrance, which might be expected of the mid-nineteenth century Picturesque. Fine finials and pendants adorn the gables. A long verandah with chamfered pillars runs along the south side of the house; originally narrow, it was widened by three feet in 1895. The house is constructed of local bright red brick with woodwork painted the appropriate period colour of Tuscan red. The front steps display cast-iron risers. The oldest chimney is a joined chimney with six flues.

Penryn Park was built for one of Port Hope's most famous citizens - Colonel Arthur Trefusis Heneage Williams. His father, John Tucker Williams, came to Canada during the War of 1812 and later settled in Port Hope to become its first Mayor. Arthur T.H. Williams was born in Port Hope in 1837. Arthur attended Upper Canada College in Toronto and Edinburgh University in Scotland. Like his father, he held many responsible positions in the town in addition to managing the family's business enterprises that included large land holdings and investments in timber and mines. His political career included being elected several times to the Ontario legislature from 1865 to 1875, and later holding the position of Conservative MP in Ottawa from 1878 to 1885.

After his marriage to Emily Seymour in 1859, Colonel A.T.H. Williams commissioned architect Edward Haycock to design his house named Penryn Park on the vast acreage adjacent to his father's house, Penryn Homestead (82 Victoria Street).

A.T.H. Williams is best remembered for his military career. He was Colonel of the 46th Regiment and saw service during the Fenian Invasion. As Commander of the Midland battalion during the Riel rebellion of 1885, he led a daring charge against the Metis that resulted in victory at Batoche, Saskatchewan.

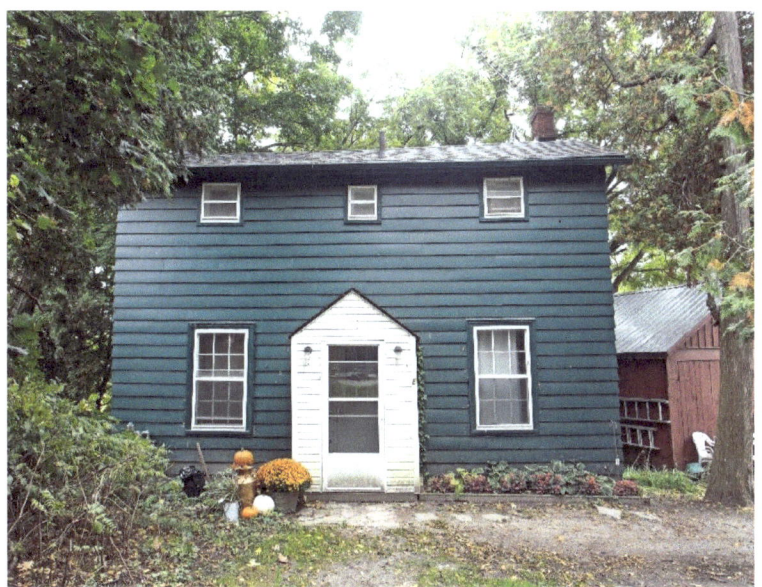

82 Victoria Street South – Winwood Lodge – c. late 1800s - Winwood Lodge was built in the middle of the last century and exhibits well the charming simplicity of an original farmhouse of the period. This small three-bay frame cottage has a very simple interior plan of two rooms upstairs and two rooms downstairs. The front door is original and is surrounded by a small, latticed porch enclosing a seat on each side. The windows are original six over six sash.

This frame house was the original farmhouse on the land that is now Penryn Park. It was moved to its present site in 1913 when Mr. H. H. King built the replacement brick farmhouse that housed the King family chauffeur. (82 Victoria Street, Penryn Park)

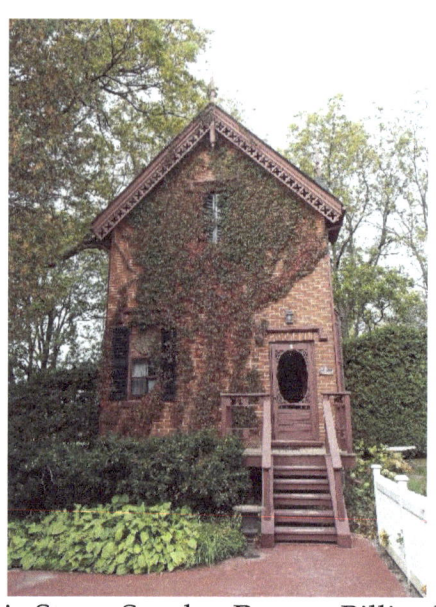

82 Victoria Street South – Penryn Billiard House – c. 1900 - This red brick building of three floors was built for Henry H. King in 1900 by local carpenter, James Tape. Its design matches that of the "Big House" with excellent bargeboard on the gables with pinnacles and drops. The one-and-a-half storey brick building has a high peaked roof and dormers that give it an unusual but charming form. The window headers and shutters are noteworthy features.

After the death of A.T.H. Williams in 1885 (his wife Emily had died in 1882) the main house was sold to Henry H. King, an American lawyer from Pittsburgh who had extensive real estate and business holdings. He became aware of the Port Hope area as one of the many Americans who spent their summers in the area. He purchased Penryn Park as his summer residence.

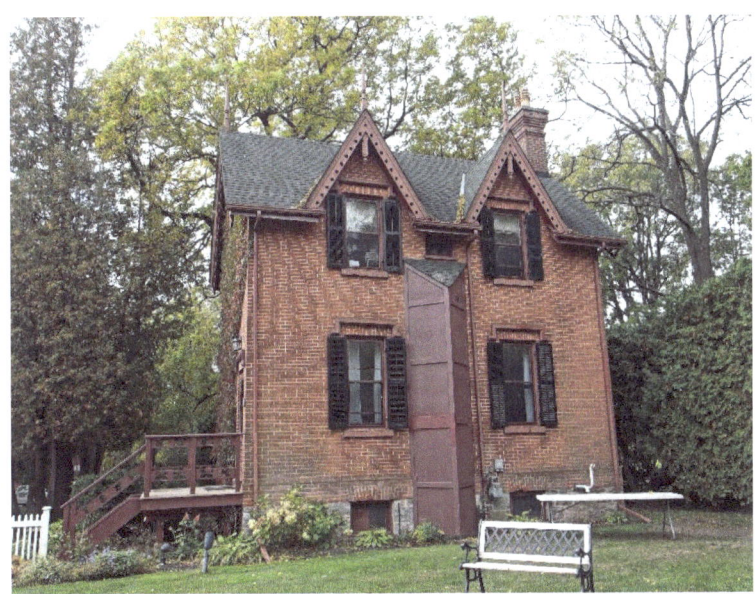

Penryn Billiard House - The door to the Billiard House had a peephole that Mr. King could use to see who was calling at the main house. The maid who answered the door would ring a bell connected to the Billiard House, and if Mr. King answered the bell, he was home, otherwise he was not available. The main floor of the building was used as a billiard room, while the upper floor housed the maid's quarters.

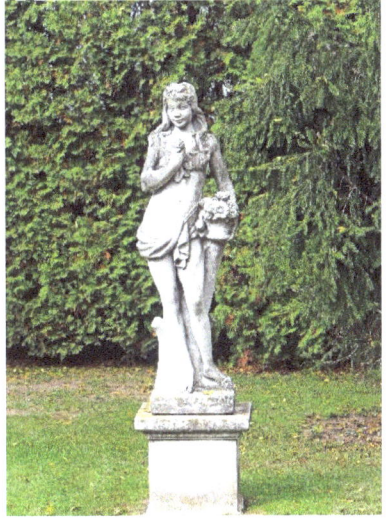

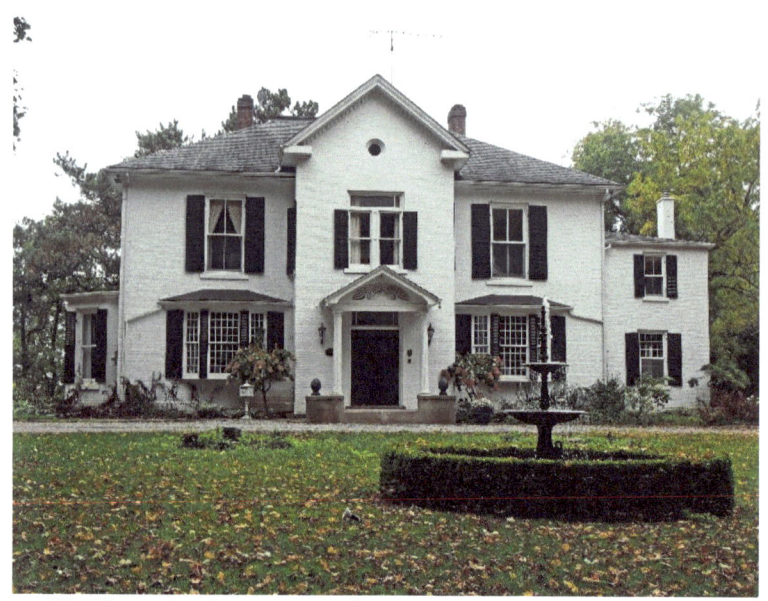

82 Victoria Street South - John Tucker Williams House (Penryn Homestead) – c. 1828-1829 - The exterior appearance is the result of extensive alterations made in the 1890s. These included the bricking over of the roughcast walls, the building of the two projecting porches to the north and south through the full height of the house, and a rebuilding of the roof, which altered its pitch and extended its eaves. The exterior double doors have a rectangular transom above them. The roof is a medium pitched hip with centre flat deck and has brick chimneys. Each of the projecting porches has returned eaves, ornamental dentils, and a small circular window below the peak. From the main facade projection extends a porch with fluted Doric pillars and a carved radiating fan decoration in the pediment. On the north front projection is a pair of shuttered casement windows, and on the north facade wall are four two-over-two double hung shuttered sash windows.

Commander John Tucker Williams (1789-1854), a British naval officer, built Penryn Homestead. Williams was formerly of the Royal Navy having fought under Nelson at the battle of Trafalgar. He came to Upper Canada during the War of 1812-15 stationed with Admiral Yeo's Fleet on Lake Ontario based at Kingston.

Penryn Homestead is one of the oldest known dwellings in Port Hope. The house was named Penryn after the area in Cornwall from which John. T. Williams came. It was built of lumber cut on the property and sawn in a water-powered mill on the Ganaraska River. Because the family was anxious to move in, the house was rushed to completion with green lumber so the family was unable to live in it the first winter due to shrinkage. Bricks for the fireplaces and chimneys were made in Port Hope in the brickyard once located south east of present-day Trinity College School.

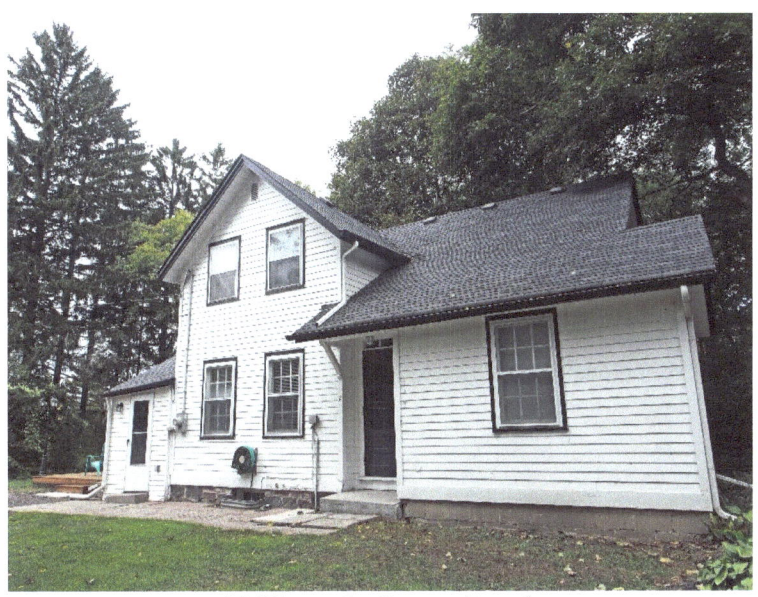

82 Victoria Street South

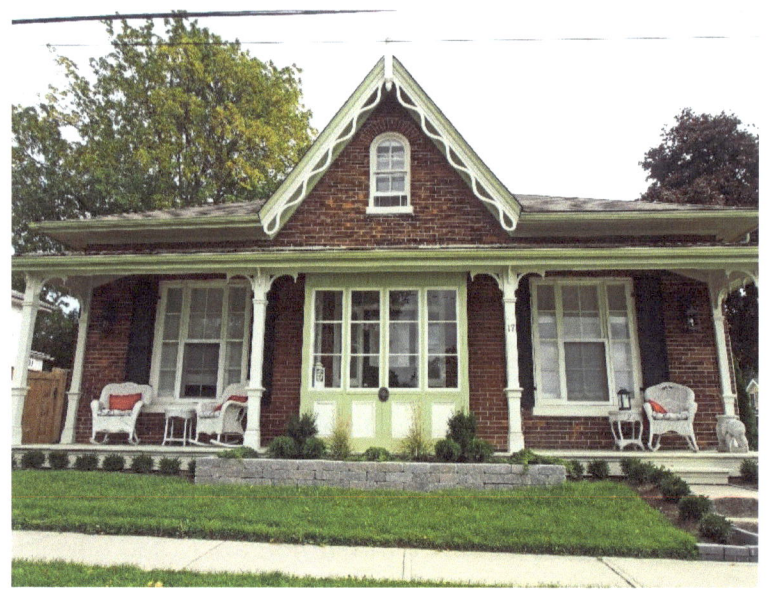

17 Victoria Street South - Samuel Coombe Cottage – c. 1860 - This is a one storey high hip-roofed Ontario cottage, roughly square in plan with an ell to the rear. Constructed in stretcher-bond brick, it stands on a level site on a corner lot. The facade is symmetrically arranged around a central front door flanked by sidelights and transom. The gable is decorated with bargeboard and accented by a round-headed window and topped by a spike finial and ornament. Of special interest is the front door vestibule that could be seasonally removed in the warmer months.

Samuel Coombe (1826-1905) was born in Stowford County, Devon England emigrating to Port Hope during the prosperous early 1850's. He made a contribution as a carpenter during the building boom, and into the following decades.

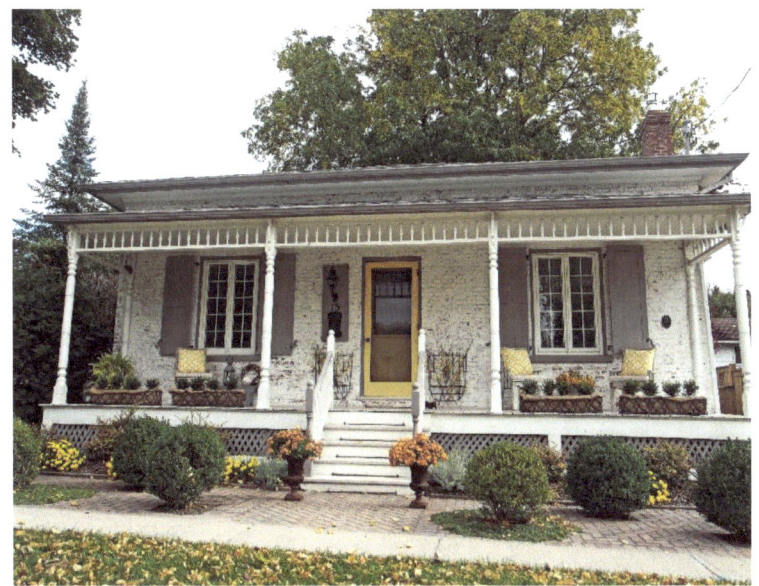

15 Victoria Street South – Greenaway Cottage - c. 1862 - The house is constructed of triple brick. William Greenaway (1819-1882) was a gentleman born in Cornwall England in 1819.

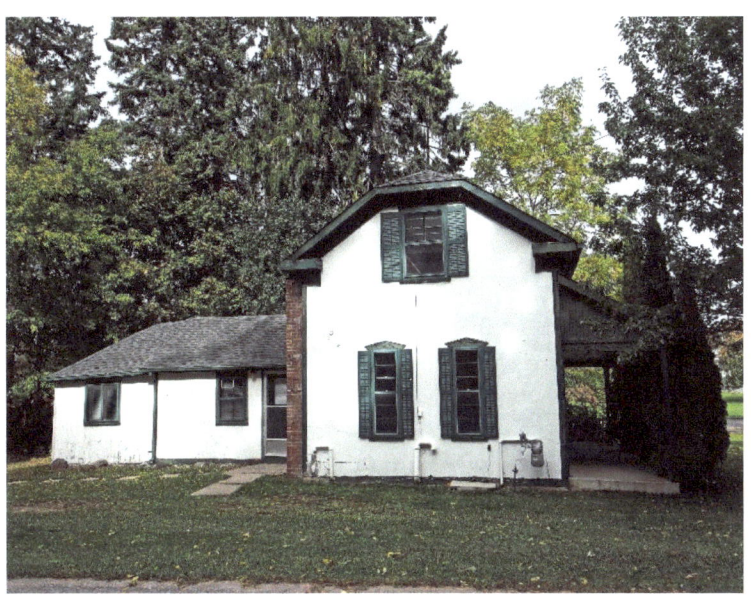

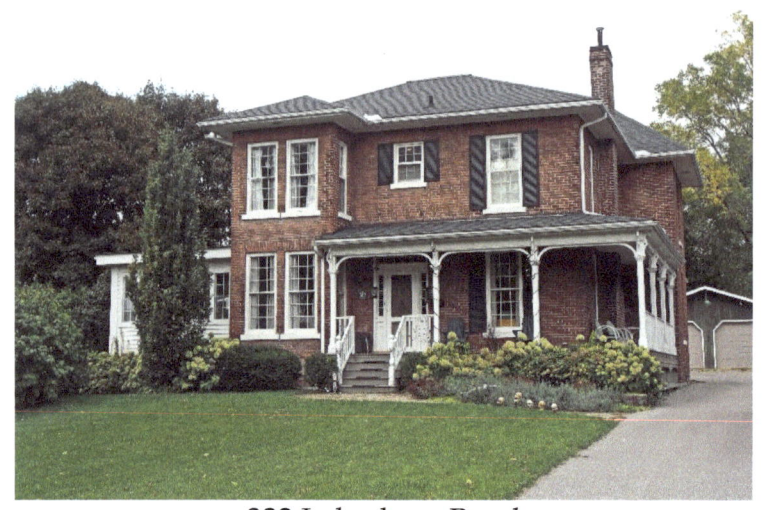

322 Lakeshore Road

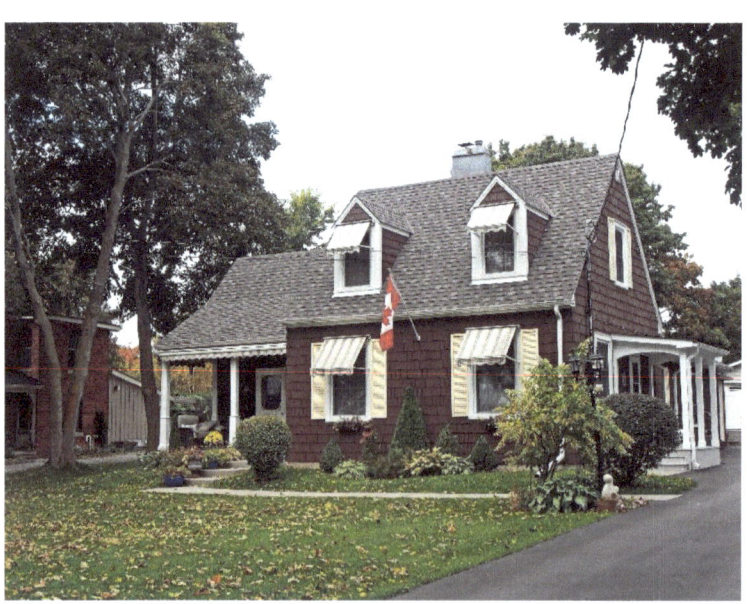

330 Lakeshore Road

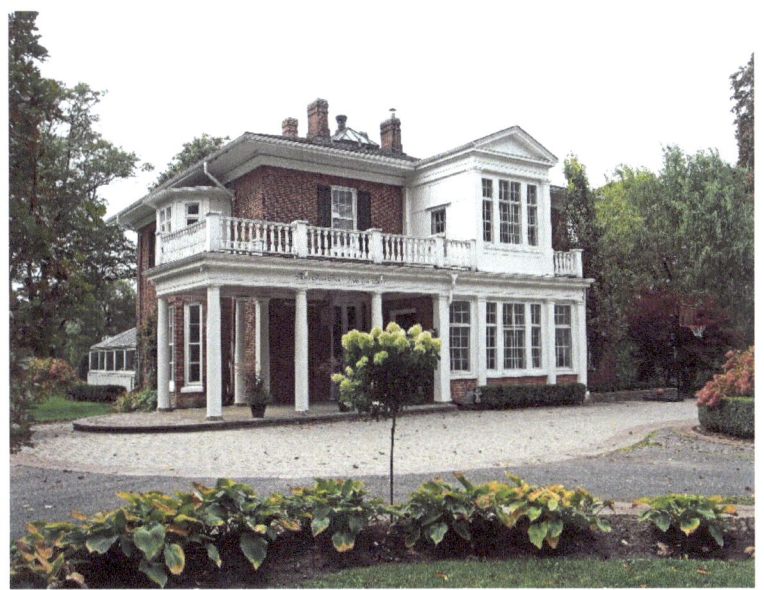

345 Lakeshore Road - William & Augusta Fraser House (Dunain) – c. 1857 - It was named Dunain (translated means Hill of the Birds) after the family's ancestral home near Inverness in Scotland. The house was built by William A. Fraser on land given by his wife's family, the Williams, owners of Penryn Homestead. In 1898, the house was taken over by Mr. Fraser's daughter, Sarah and her husband, Frederick Barlow Cumberland. The Cumberland coat of arms etched on stained glass graces the front entrance window.

The style of the original house is Loyalist Georgian with its dignified symmetry but this house exhibits a breakaway from the rigid symmetry of earlier Georgian houses. The porch and portico were added to the north side in the latter part of the century, as was the conservatory to the south, which was rebuilt again in the early part of the 20th century. The original portion of the house is a two-storey red brick structure with a symmetrically placed front door, and symmetrically placed windows.

The roof is a hip roof with wide overhangs and bold cornice fascia. The roof culminates in a glass roofed Belvedere bringing light into the central hall below. There is a west wing, probably originally servants' quarters constructed in the same manner as the main house and capped by a Belvedere, lighting the centre hall of this wing. A further addition was made to this west wing to accommodate a more modern kitchen, constructed in a similar manner to the original house.

In the latter part of the 19th century, the front portico and porch were added to the north side of the house, the style of which is more Classic Revival popular in that period.

The porch is a good example of the classical period with classical Doric columns and a wide entablature and in-filled with large windows extending to the ceiling inside. These windows are an eight over sixteen central window with four over eight sidelights on both floors, and sides of the portico and panelled. The railing for the upper porch completes this classical composition. To the southeast is a conservatory constructed in steel and is an excellent example of early 20th century greenhouse construction. This present structure replaces an earlier conservatory.

When Augusta Williams, daughter of J.T. Williams, married William Fraser in 1857, they were given a parcel of land severed from her father's estate, Penryn Homestead (82 Victoria Street South). William Fraser (1821-1894), originally from Inverness Scotland, came to Canada in 1840, and Port Hope in 1846, as the representative of a group of Montreal merchants. In 1859, William Fraser became the first elected Mayor of Port Hope and held a number of prestigious positions throughout his career including agent for Canada Western Assurance, director of the Bank of Toronto, stockholder of the Midland Loan and Savings Company, advocate of the Midland Railway, and active member of the militia as Captain of the 46th Battalion.

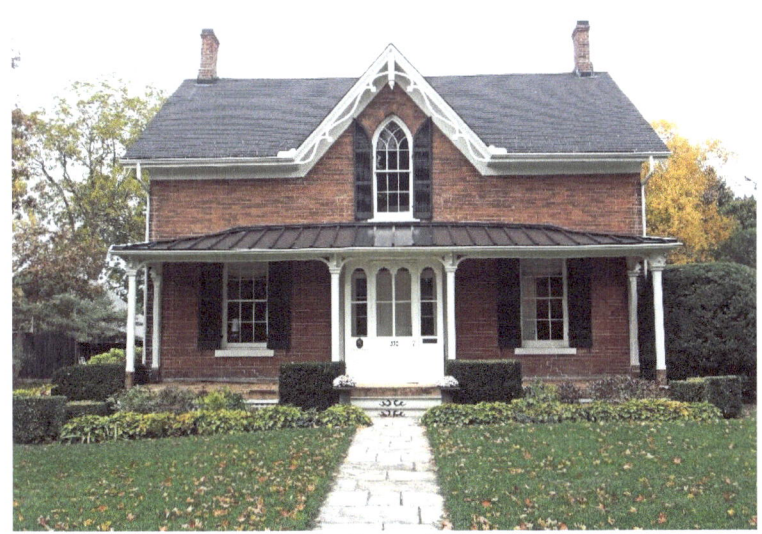

350 Lakeshore Road - Brand Farmhouse – c. 1860 – It was built by Daniel Brand, a local farmer. It is a fine example of a 1½ storey brick Victorian Revival Ontario Farmhouse. The house form has symmetrical placement of six over six double hung windows on either side of the entrance. The frame front door vestibule is intact, and is a good example of this important element of early houses in Ontario. This vestibule was seasonably removable and behind, the existing front door with sidelights is intact. A frame front porch extends the full width of the house with decorative columns and fretwork and a metal roof typical of these original porches. The house has a simple gable roof with symmetrical chimneys and a high, pitched dormer with a lacy bargeboard trim. In the centre of the gable is a beautiful Gothic window with a fine example of Gothic tracery.

Daniel Brand was born in Suffolk, England in 1791. He came to Canada and was granted crown land in Lot 15, Concession 1 in 1842. Jonathan was born in 1807 in Suffolk, England. He initially emigrated to Vermont where he married his wife, Pamela Ford.

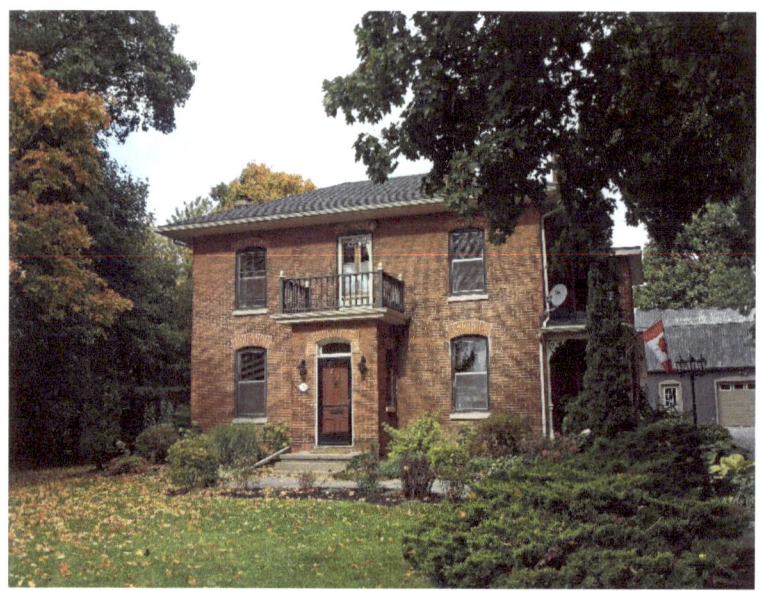

332 Lakeshore Road

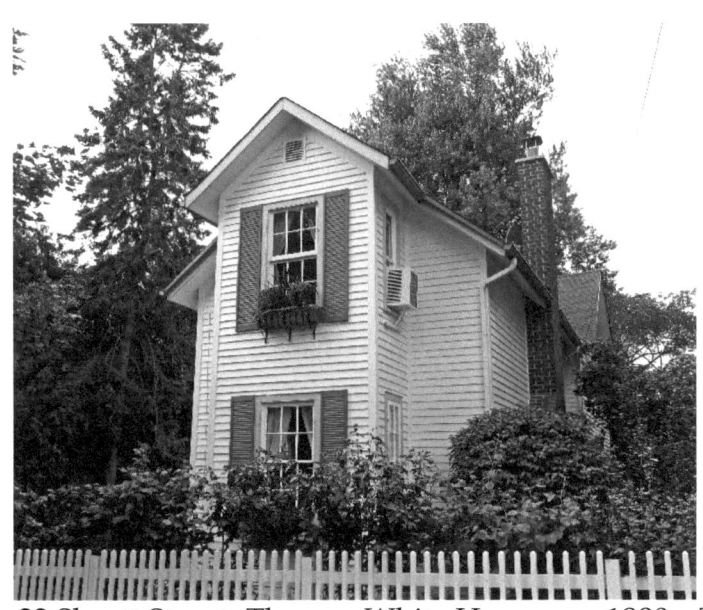

22 Shortt Street -Thomas White House – c. 1890 – The style of this frame two-storey house can be described as cottage with horizontal wood ship lap siding, six over six windows and simple trim. The plan is unusual with a side entrance accentuated by a simple but elegant porch. High pitched cross axis roofs add particular interest to this house. The front of the house has a picket fence.

White was originally from England, born in 1838, and as of the 1881 census had four daughters and one son.

The house remained in the White family for many decades transferring to the White children in 1929.

In 1836, Reverend Jonathan Shortt became Rector of St. Mark's Church, formerly St. John's (51 King Street), and he took over Reverend Coghlan's teaching duties at the grammar school. The naming of Shortt Street commemorates Reverend Jonathan Shortt who conducted the services at St. Mark's Church from 1836-67.

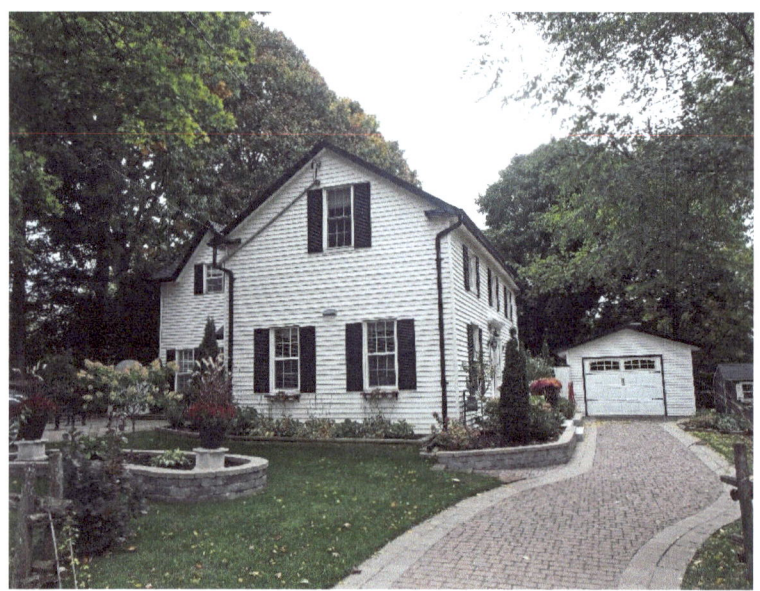

Shortt Street

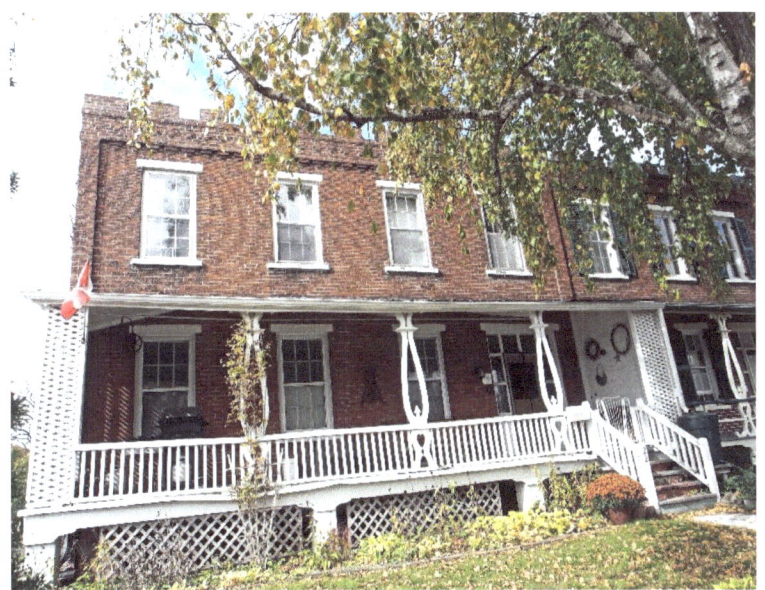

22 Barrett Street - Barrett's Terrace – c. 1860 - This west end section of Barrett's Terrace is a fine, well-preserved and maintained house. With four bays to the main facade, it is larger than the rest of the row houses, apart from the one at the east end. The battlemented parapet, six over six double-hung sash, door case with sidelights and transom, and trellised verandah with lyre-shaped supports are all original details.

Along with adjacent mills and the nearby Octagon House, Barrett's Terrace is part of the legacy of William Barrett and his family, a prominent miller and entrepreneur in Port Hope in the last half of the 19th century. William Barrett Jr. built Barrett's Terrace to provide accommodations for the English labourers and their families brought to Canada to work in his nearby mill. In 1856, Barrett built his residence, Port Hope's unique example of an Octagon House, located directly north of Barrett's Terrace on Martha Street.

William Barrett (1784-1861) left Bathpoole, Cornwall, England in 1831 to launch a milling operation in Canada. In England, his family owned an established milling enterprise. He made the journey to Canada along with his wife Elizabeth and children. Barrett built two factories, one on either side of the river at Barrett Street. The mills included a sawmill, and wagon and carriage making business with a blacksmith shop, and grist and flour mills. There was a bedstead and chair factory, and carding and cloth-dressing establishment. Mr. Barrett also leased workshops to other business enterprises. The descendants of William Barrett carried on the operation of the mills into the early 1900s. William Barrett Jr. (1817-1875) operated the mills with his father, and then his son, Harold (1858-1908) succeeded him.

While the row houses were originally built to house Barrett's mill workers, the terrace later became a desirable residence for young families.

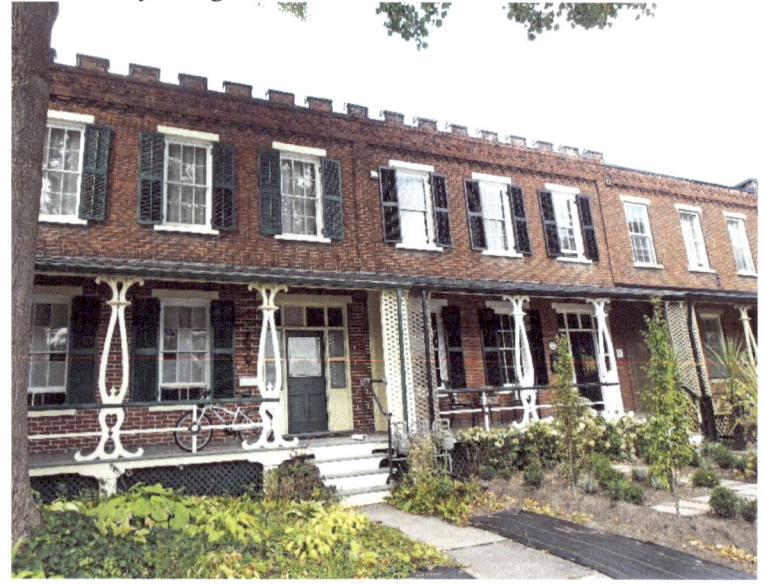

24 Barrett Street – It has three bays on the front facade, the original sash and door case, a battlemented parapet, and a trellis verandah with lyre supports; shutters added.

26 Barrett Street - The building is notable for its disciplined and ordered facade, its battlemented parapet, and original door case and window sash and fine verandah of lyre design.

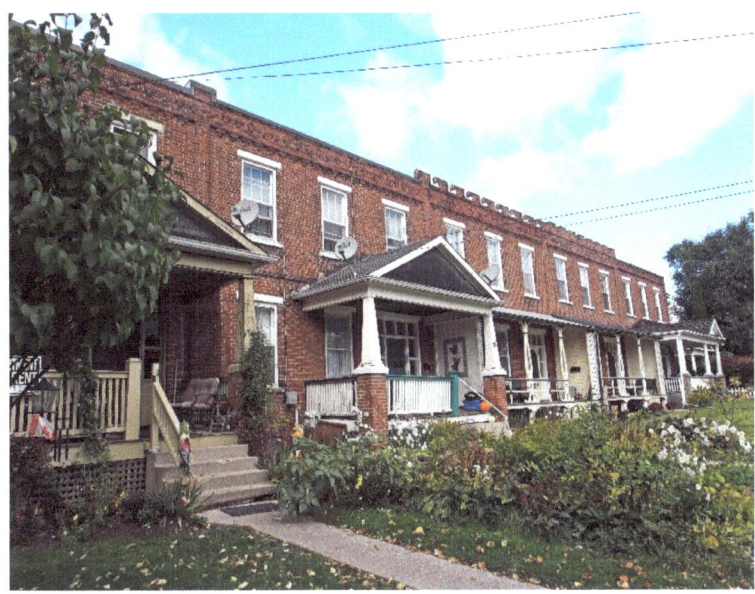

32-40 Barrett Street

36-38 Barrett Street - The porch has lyre shaped tracery. The main structure is brick with an intricate brick pattern at the cornice. Large symmetrically placed six over six double hung windows and a handsome door and sidelight are notable.

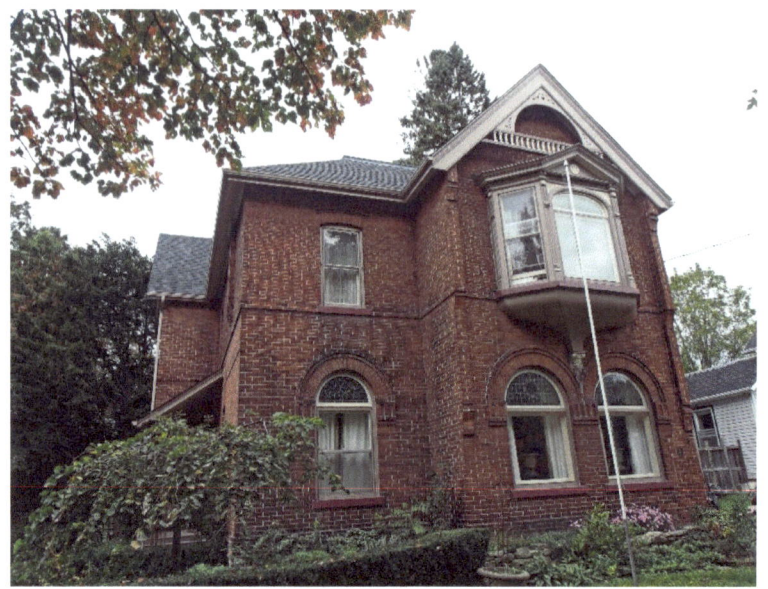

48 Bloomsgrove Avenue - Thomas B. Chalk House – c. 1890 - This late Victorian two-storey brick house has fine brick detailing. The centre bay of the house has two large arched windows (typical of the Romanesque style) with stained glass semicircular transoms. Above is a protruding bay window in frame with fine wood detailing and a large arched top central window. The peak of the roof above has decorative fretwork suggesting a more Edwardian period. The side bay has a similar arched top window.

On either side of the house is a porch. The west porch protects the front door located on the side of the building, while the east porch provides a kitchen entrance. Each of these porches has decorative columns and fretwork. A side bay window is similar to the front bay window. The brickwork has decorative brick arches over windows, brick corbels with specially formed brick, brick banding, and decorative brick chimneys.

Thomas Butterfield Chalk, son of Robert Chalk, owner of the Chalk Carriage Works was the owner of this property for nearly 20 years. Robert Chalk (1820-1890), an English immigrant born in Biddeford, Devonshire, England, settled in Port Hope in 1842 and established a wagon and carriage-making business. Chalk Carriage Works (46 Cavan Street) was located on Cavan Street on the steep hill where South and Cavan Street meet, a hill that was sometimes referred to as Chalk's Hill.

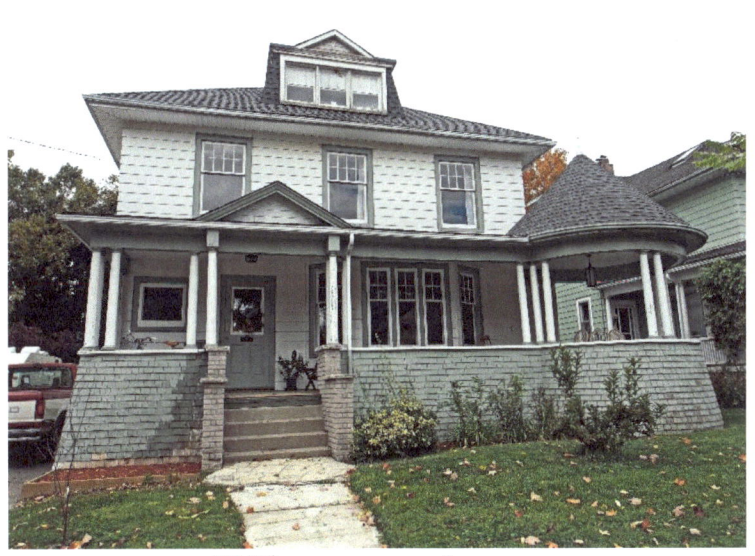

52 Bloomsgrove Avenue

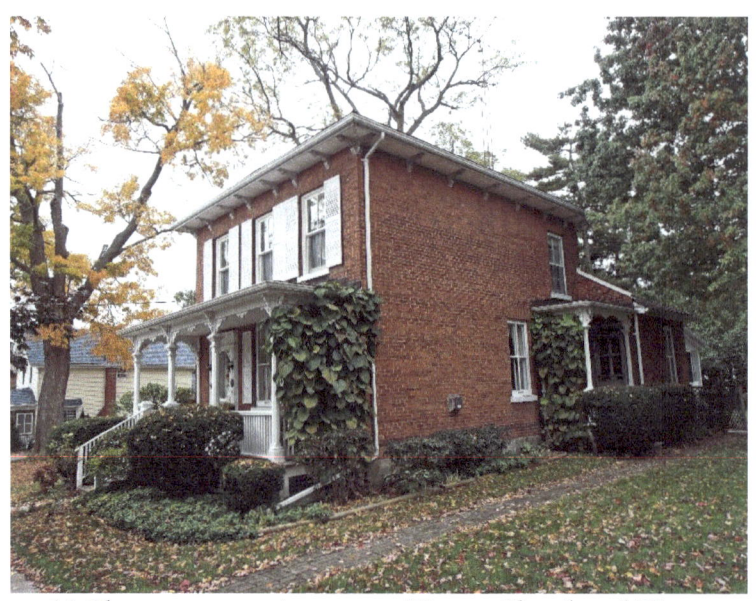

44 Bloomsgrove Avenue - Henry Shepherd House – c. 1875 - This is a two-storey brick residence with a hipped roof. It has a three-bay façade. The side hall plan places the front door at the left. Windows are regularly spaced under flat arches and glazed with two over two sash. Louvred shutters add to the facade composition. Of special note is the verandah with its slender, chamfered posts (note collar trim) and restrained use of gingerbread. Railing with plain squared balusters is a handsome detail. The same pattern appears on a small stoop verandah at the rear.

Henry Shepherd was a merchant grocer who was in partnership with Thompson Ballagh, a baker operating under the business name of Ballagh and Shepherd. Ballagh and Shepherd were located on Walton (118-120 Walton Street).

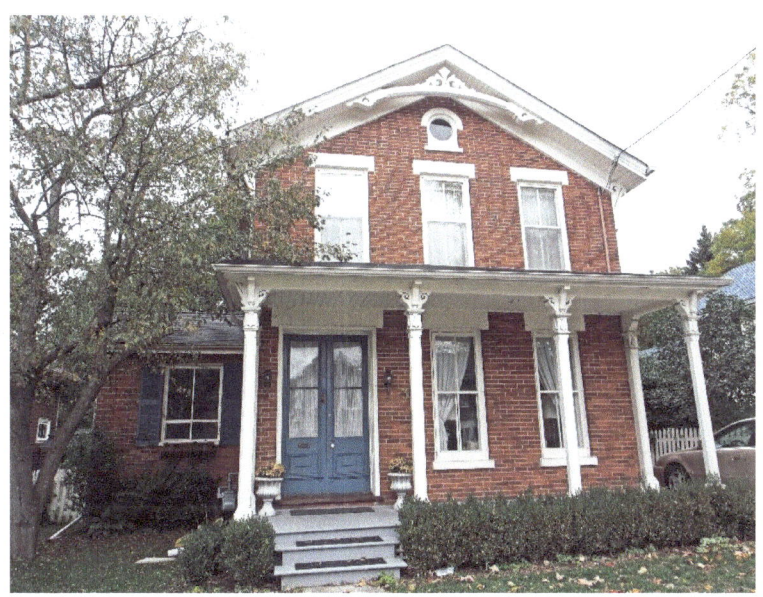

36 Bloomsgrove Avenue

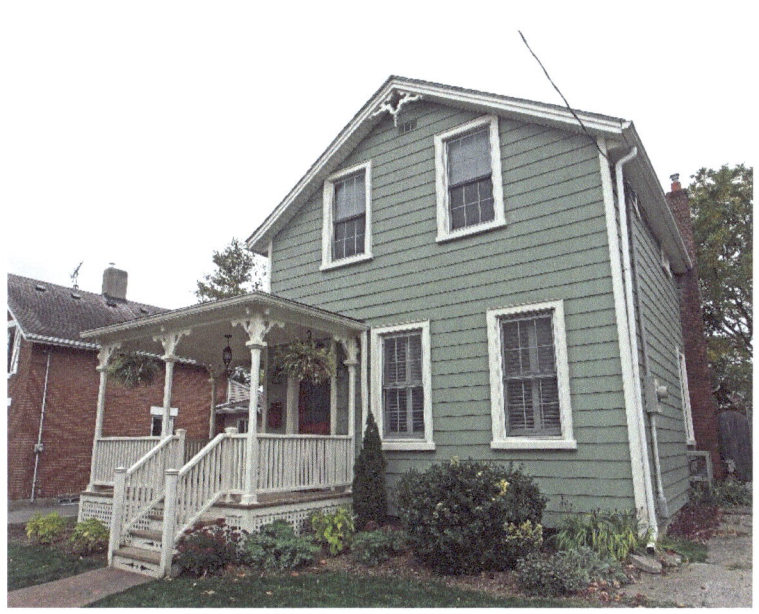

30 Bloomsgrove Avenue

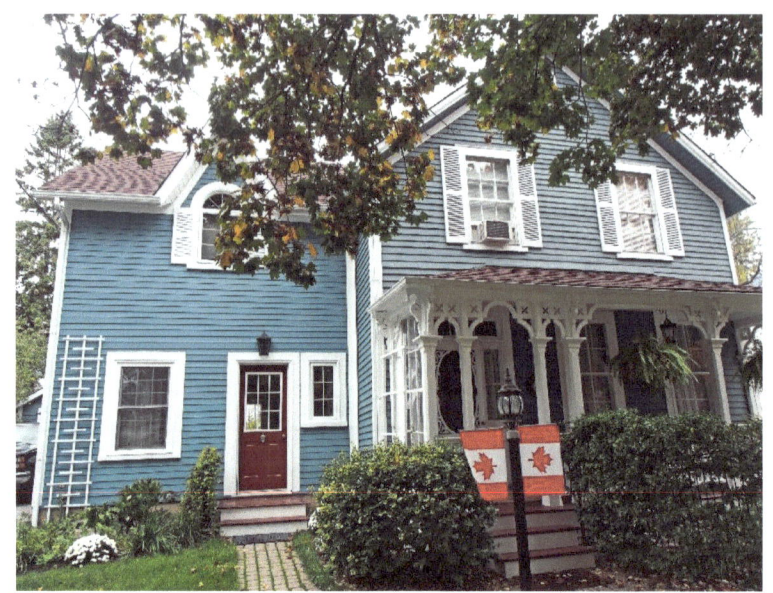

Bloomsgrove Avenue

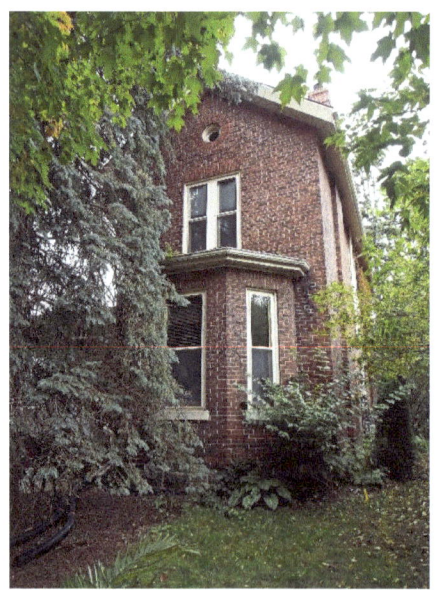

Bloomsgrove Avenue

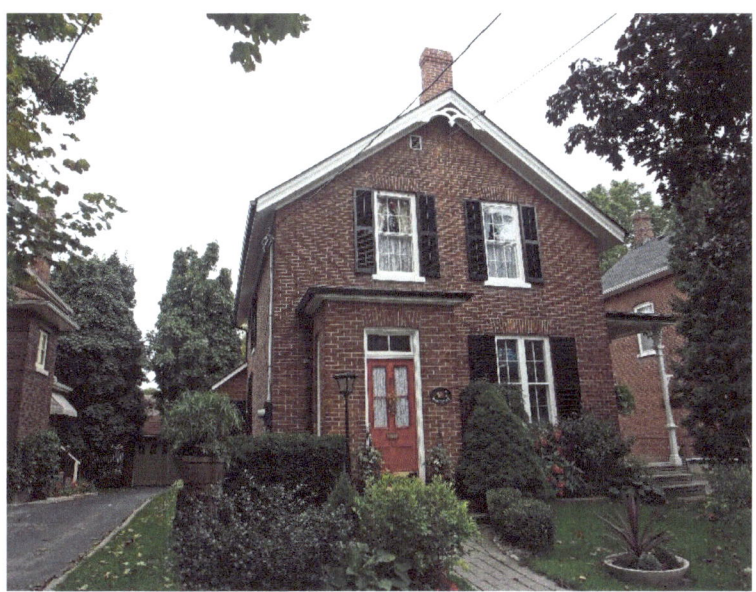

5 Bloomsgrove Avenue - Robert Horsey House – c. 1870
- This one and a half storey, two bay house is rectangular in plan and constructed of brick veneer laid in stretcher bond with a coarse rubble foundation. The roof is a high gable, gable end to the street, and contains some decorative trim at the apex. The eaves consist of a plain boxed cornice. The shuttered windows on the upper storey are six over six double-hung sash with plain surround and lugsills. The decorative details on the porch are Victorian details.

Robert Horsey was a Port Hope carpenter.

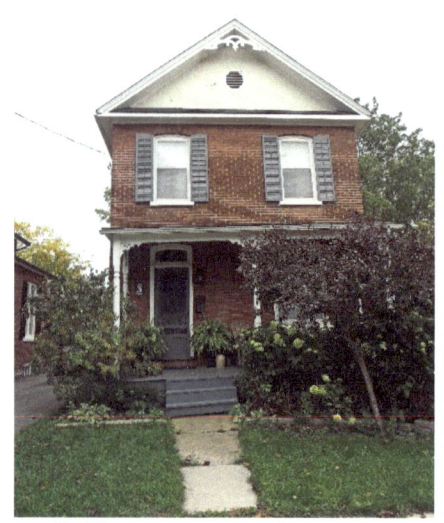

3 Bloomsgrove Avenue

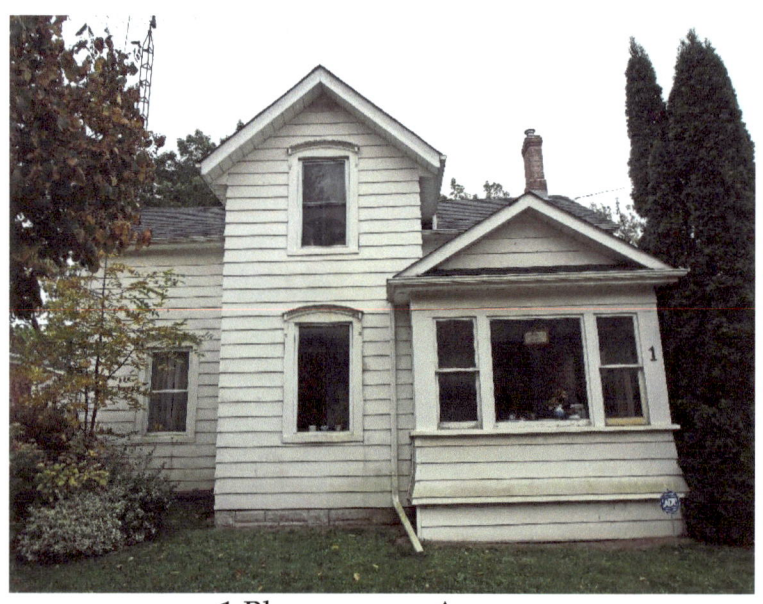

1 Bloomsgrove Avenue

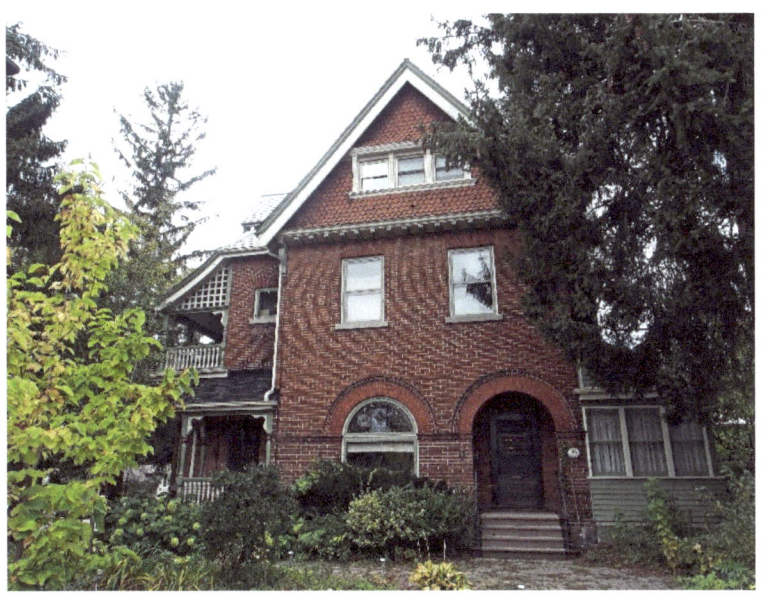

98 Ontario Street - Thomas Wickett House (Penstowe) – c. 1894 - Although built in the Queen Anne Revival style, it has detailing of the Romanesque style. The roof is irregular and complicated, but is composed basically of several steeply pitched gables and one overhanging gable dormer. The gables are pedimented with some rafters exposed. The pediment has a set of triple windows in a bold wooden surround. Trimming the windows are tooled pilasters and heavy entablature. Decorative shingles complete the pediment.

The stretcher-bond brick house has various types of structural openings from flat on the top storey, to segmental on the projecting south bay, to rounded Romanesque on the front facade. Voussoirs head most windows, but protruding arched gables of brick surround the semi-elliptical openings. Stringer courses join the sills of the house and join the tips of the arches on the main facade. The main door is set in one of the arched openings, but is itself flat.

Another striking feature of the house is a second-storey bell-cast balcony adorned with heavy turned balusters and turned columns. The balcony roof is supported by brackets and has a molded frieze. The open end of the balcony is partially filled by lattice-like woodwork. The spooled columns are turned and have a rounded, bulbous appearance. On the first storey, a shed-roofed porch with the same characteristics can be seen. The house sits on a squared-stone foundation with segmental basement windows.

Thomas Wickett was born in Cornwall, England in 1849. He and his family including his mother Eliza and brother John emigrated to Canada. Thomas and John Wickett established a dry goods store that was situated in several locations on Walton Street (Tempest Block 62-68 Walton Street, Quinlan Block 78-92 Walton Street). Thomas married Mary Ellen Jenkins in September 1881.

George Martell Miller, a notable Toronto architect designed the house. Miller was born in Port Hope in 1854, and educated at the University of Toronto in architecture.

The Wicketts named the house Penstowe after the area they were originally from in Cornwall.

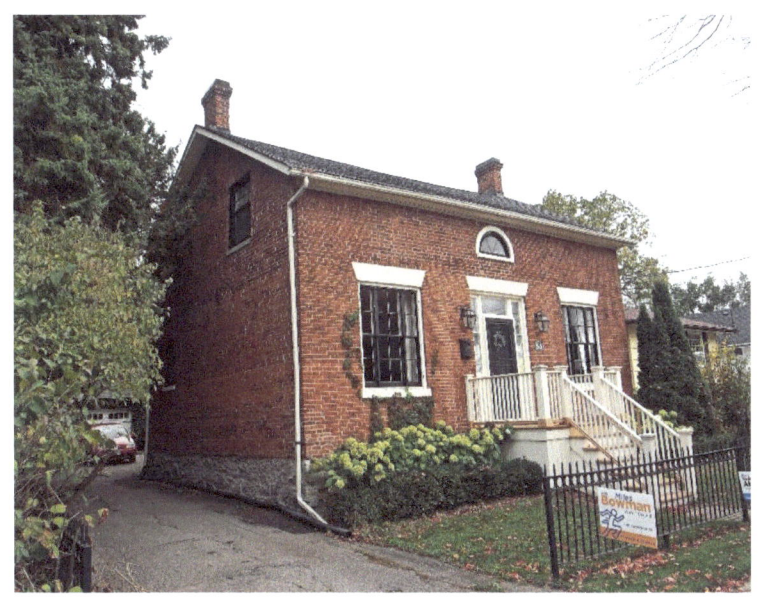

53 Hope Street North

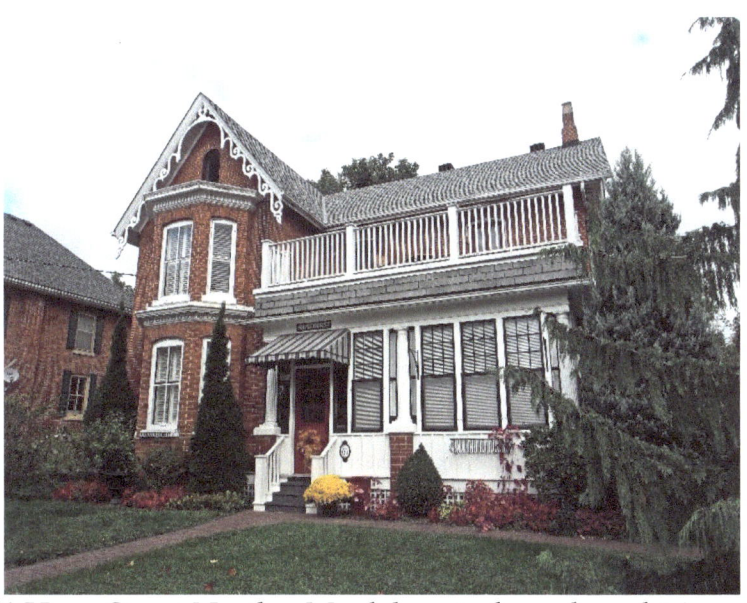

61 Hope Street North – Maplehurst – bargeboard trim on
gable above two-storey bay window

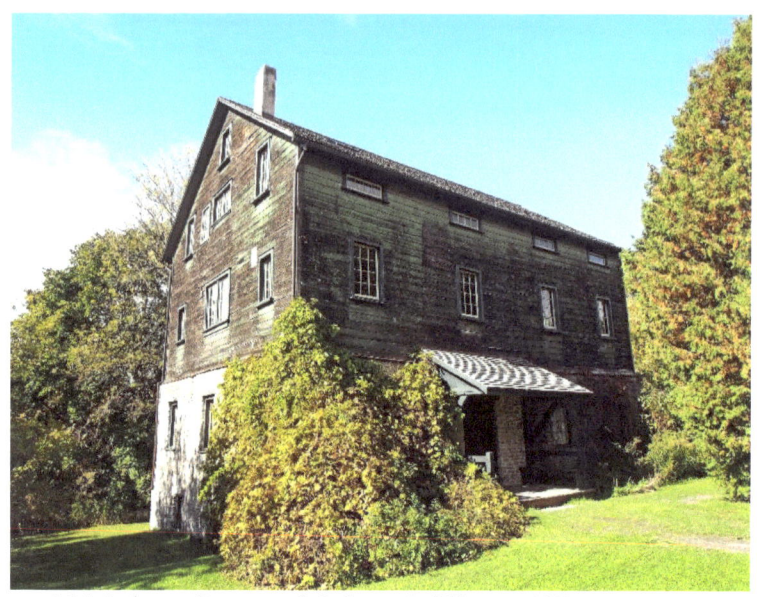

46 Molson Street - Molson Mill – c. 1851 - It is a typical heavy timber frame gristmill in the functional tradition. The Molson Mill is of post and beam construction rising three and a half stories above a foundation comprised of river rock. The gable roof is finished in original style cedar shingles.

The Molson name is synonymous with brewing and distilleries in Canada, being one of the oldest manufacturing enterprises dating back to the eighteenth century. The Montreal based family also owned steamships, railways, and the Molson Bank, which would later merge with the Bank of Montreal in 1925. Based in Montreal, Thomas Molson, son of the founder, John Molson, wanted to expand into Upper Canada. He applied to York for a permit to build a brewery, but was rejected due to local competition.

In 1851, Port Hope was the next largest port in Upper Canada, so Thomas Molson purchased property about a mile from the business part of town near Cavan and Jocelyn Streets on the Ganaraska River. The purchase included a brewery, Crawford's distillery, a flour mill, a sawmill, a stave factory, a millpond and dam as well as a wharf and warehouse on the lake.

Molson steamships were used to transport malt barley in large quantities. During the Molson tenure in Port Hope, more barley was exported from the town than any other port. Robert Orr managed the mills reporting to Thomas Molson daily. He resided in the nearby Molson Mill House (285 Hope Street North).

The Molson Mill was used as the flour mill – it had six runs of stones and was capable of turning out 300 barrels of flour a day. The saw mill turned out 6,000 feet of lumber a day, and there was also on the premises an excellent stave factory for the manufacturing of flour barrel staves capable of making 7,000 staves a day. The mills also included a lath and picket factory, and a planing machine.

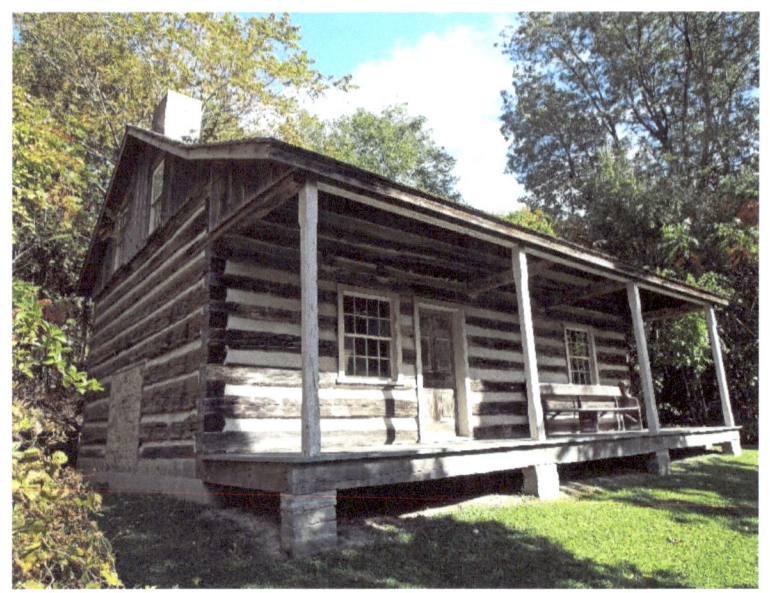

Log cabin near mill

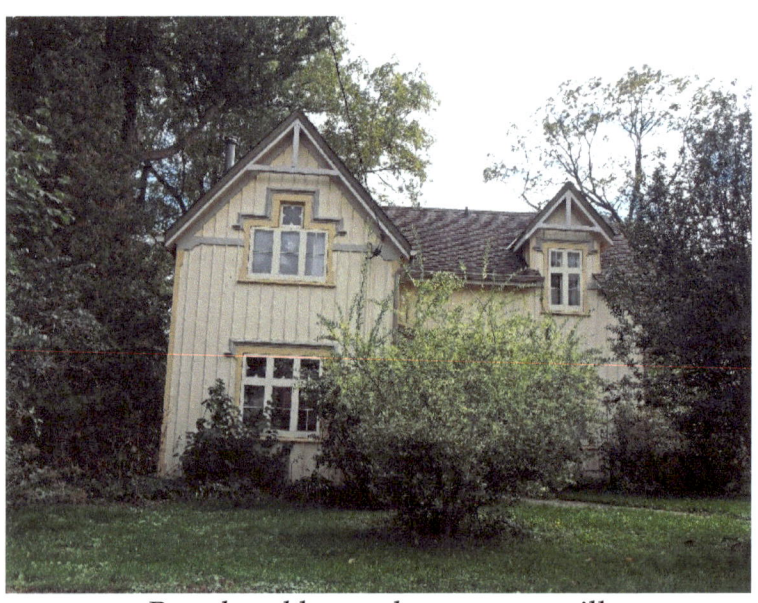

Board and batten house near mill

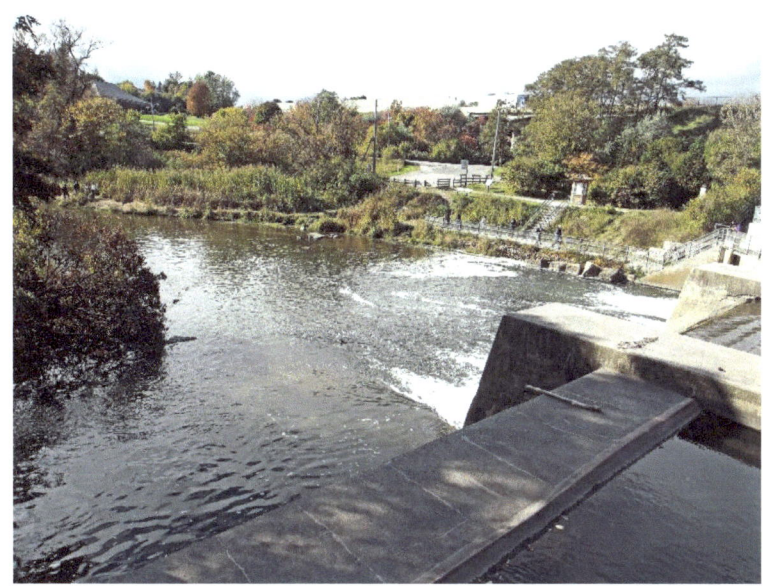

Dam

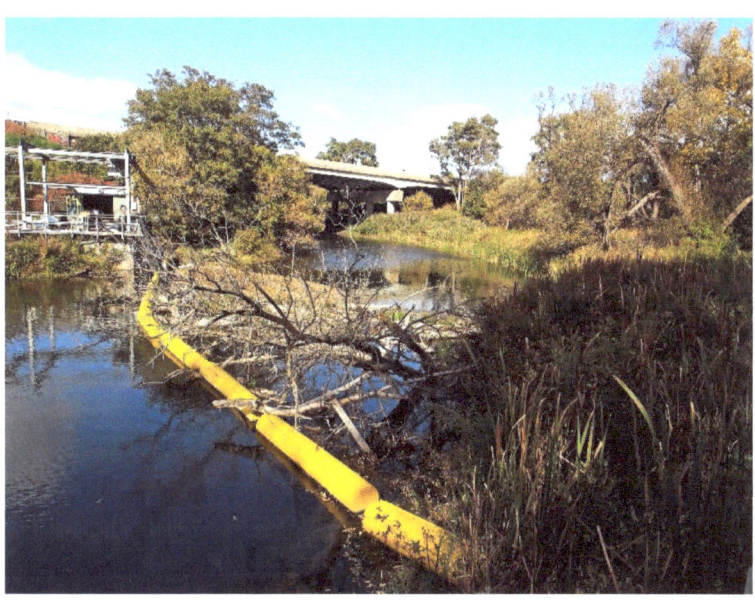

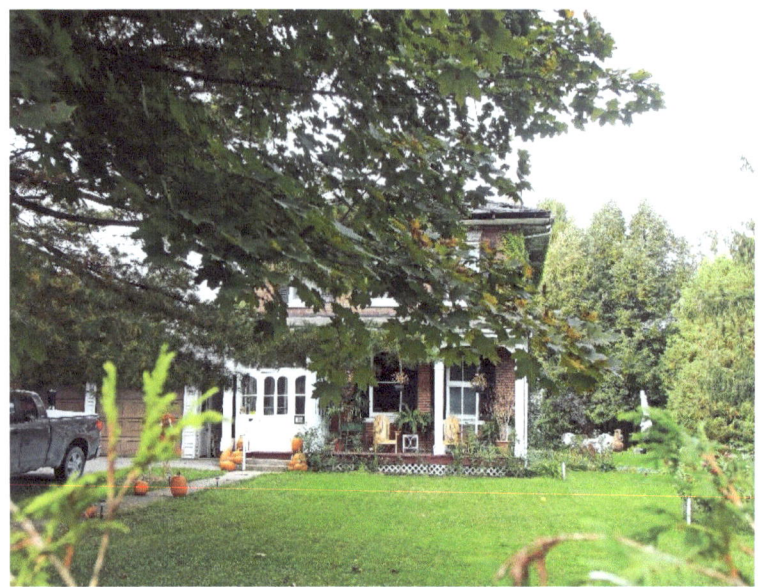

36 William Street - William Stevenson House – c. 1867 - The house, in the Classical Revival style, is a three bay, two-storey, side hall plan with hip roof, wide eaves and originally an encircling verandah. Of special interest is the front door vestibule of the verandah which provided additional seasonal protection from the elements.

William Stevenson Sr. (1796-1893) was born in County Fermanagh, Ireland and immigrated to Port Hope in 1840 with his wife Mary and son, William Godfrey Stevenson. William G. Stevenson (1833 - 1914) was born in Ireland in 1833.

William G. Stevenson appears in Port Hope business directories by 1871 as a tailor residing on William Street.

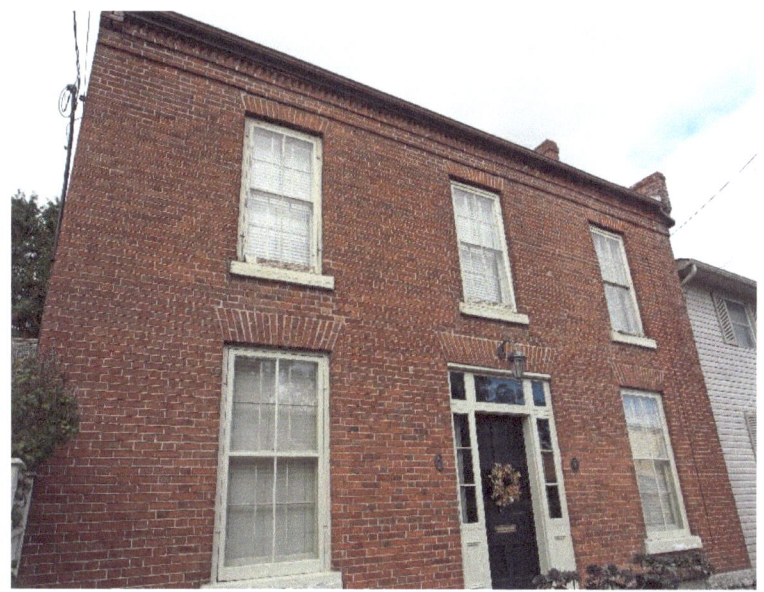

6 William Street - John Adams Townhouse – c. 1850 - This house is a fine example of the urban townhouse style characterized by blind parapet walls and a two storey three bay facade. 6 William Street is constructed of brick laid in Flemish bond, with windows headed by radiating voussoirs. The front entrance has recessed sidelights and transom divided by two mullions. The six-over-six double-hung sash windows are headed by radiating brick voussoirs and have lugsills of wood.

John Adams was a bricklayer.

In 1854, the house and lot were sold to John Might, Port Hope saddler, harness, and trunk maker. John Might (1794-1865) was originally from Dublin, Ireland emigrating to Canada in 1833. In addition to his business enterprise, he also performed the function of the Justice of the Peace and was a quartermaster in the militia in 1847.

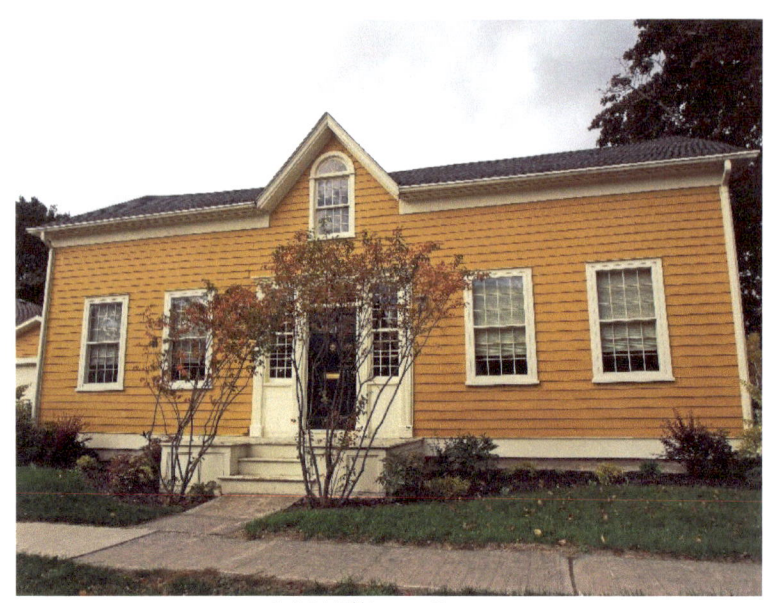

24 William Street

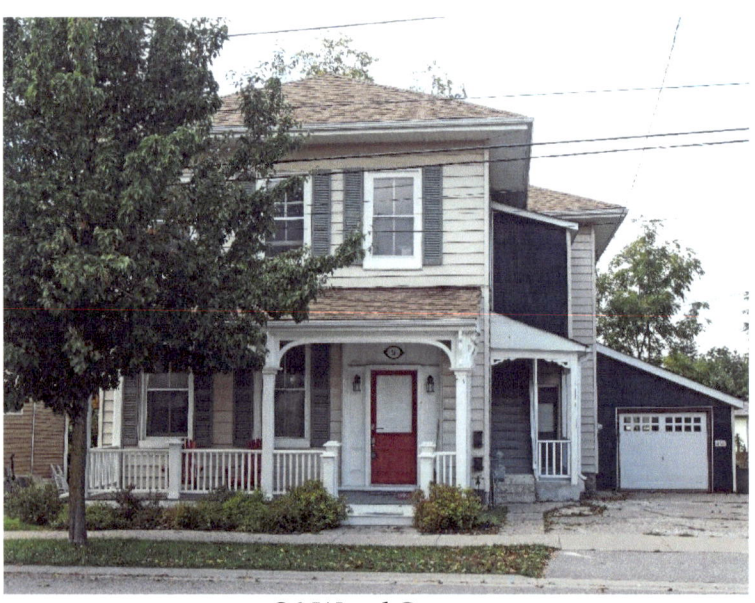

26 Ward Street

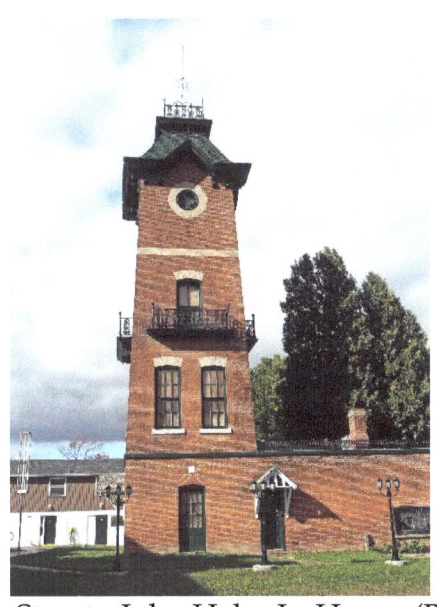

162 Peter Street - John Helm Jr. House (Belgrave) Water Tower – c. 1877 - The water tower is four storeys high made entirely of original bricks kilned on the estate property. The first three levels have large rectangular windows. Some windows are fenced in by elaborate wrought iron balustrades, which came from the nearby iron foundry owned by Mr. Helm. The uppermost level of the tower has circular spoked windows set back within decorative light-coloured brickwork. The glass windowpanes themselves (some still original) are also said to have been made on the property. For a finishing touch of English grace, the tower is crowned with a green gabled roof with a widow's walk. Inside the tower, there is a wooden spiral staircase, which winds its way up to the fourth level. The well beneath the tower, which is brick lined all the way down, was some seventy-five feet deep and about ten feet in diameter.

John Helm Jr. (1816-1912) built the water tower in 1877 as part of his thirty-acre estate called Belgrave. The tower concealed a large storage tank capable of pumping and storing a large quantity of lake water. A five-thousand-gallon wooden pressure vessel rested on the fourth level of this tower. Originally, its purpose was to supply the house and surrounding acreage with water. Five acres were irrigated by an underground piping system used to water the lawns and gardens. But in the event of a fire, there was a readily available source of water. In addition to the header system, a storage tank was built over the attic of the mansion. Whenever the tower water level went down, a cantilever device automatically switched over to the attic tank.

John Helm Jr. was a prominent local businessman who established a foundry and machine shop on Mill Street in 1849, capable of making steam engines, boilers, threshing machines, and reaping machines. The foundry was later located at Queen and Peter Streets powered by Helm's Dam on the Ganaraska River. He learned the trade from his father, John Helm Sr. at his father's foundry on College Street in Cobourg.

In 1872, the Town recognized the need for a municipal waterworks that could supply water by use of rotary pump using local water power supplied through a series of underground pipes to assist in fire fighting. John Helm offered to install the system and completed the work in 1875. A water works building was built adjacent to Helm's Dam containing rotary pumps and turbines. The new waterworks system greatly enhanced fire-fighting efforts in the town.

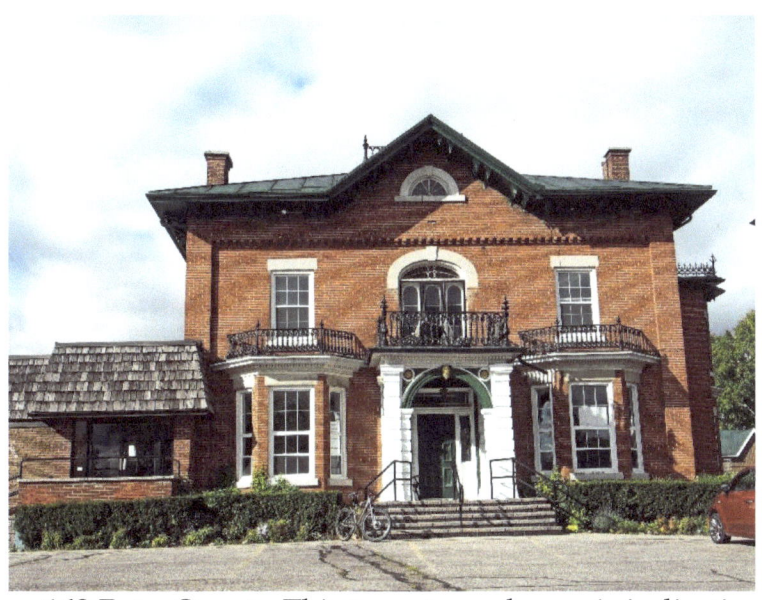

162 Peter Street - This two-storey house is indicative of the Italianate Style Victorian house. A symmetrically placed entrance is noted for its heavily decorated portico topped by iron balustrade made in the foundry of the original owner. The entrance is flanked by two bay windows with similar iron topping. The roof overhangs are supported by brackets typical of this Italianate period and is topped by a widow's walk. The semi-circular window over the entrance designed in a Florentine pattern is of particular interest. Another interesting point is the unusual width of the overhanging eaves with their double brackets.

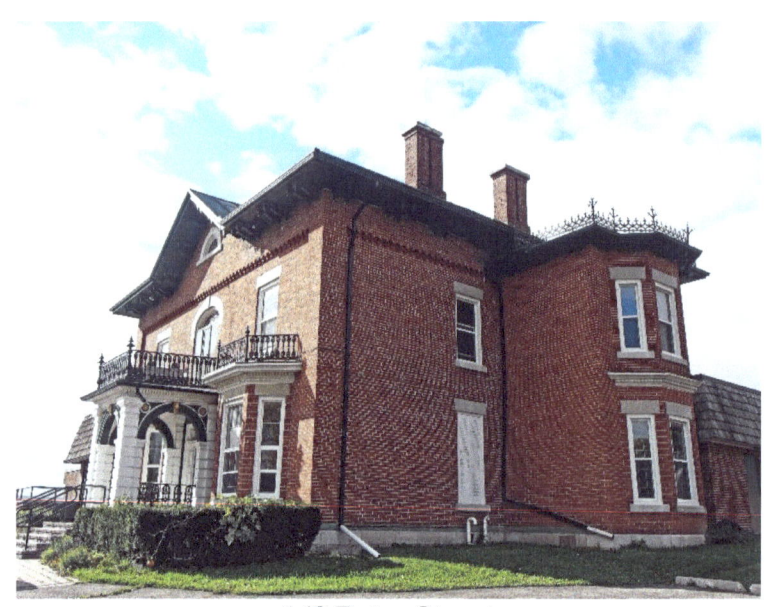

162 Peter Street

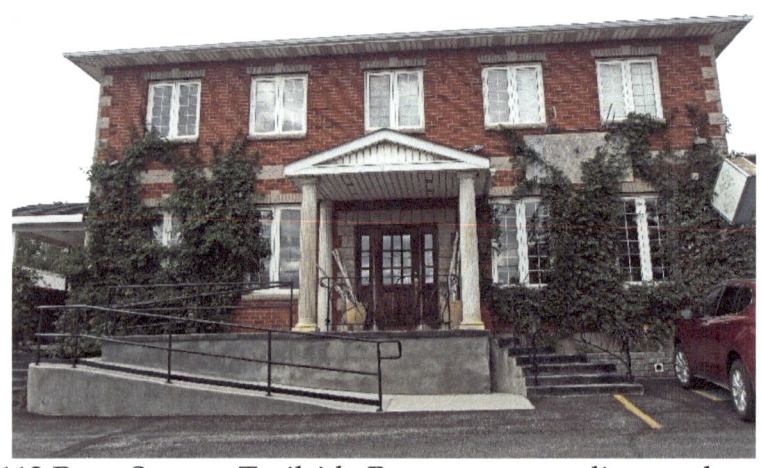

112 Peter Street – Trailside Restaurant – pediment above
entrance porch supported by Doric columns

# Other Books by Barbara Raue

Coins of Gold
Arrows, Indians and Love
The Life and Times of Barbara
The Cromwell Family Book
Laura Secord Discovered
Daddy Where Are You?

Montana Series
Book 1: Montana Dream
Book 2: Life on the Montana Frontier
Book 3: Montana to Boston and Back
Book 4: Montana Sons Go to War
Book 5: Montana Sons Return from War

Book 1: Rite of Passage
Book 2: Rite of Marriage

This is a link to Barbara's website to view all of her books
http://barbararaue.ca

# Series Name: Cruising Ontario, Saving Our History One Photo at a Time in colour photos

Books Available in Alphabetical Order:
Aberfoyle, Acton, Ajax, Alton, Amherstburg, Ancaster, Arthur, Auburn, Aylmer, Ayr, Beaver Valley, Belfountain, Belgrave, Belleville, Bloomingdale, Blyth, Brantford, Brockville, Burford, Burgessville, Burlington, Caledon, Caledonia, Cambridge, Carlow, Cayuga, Chatsworth, Cheltenham, Clifford, Colborne, Collingwood, Conestogo, Delhi, Dorchester to Aylmer, Drayton, Drumbo, Dundas, Dunlop, Dunnville, Eden Mills, Elmira, Elora, Embro, Erin, Essex, Fergus, Fort Erie, Georgetown, Goderich, Grimsby, Guelph, Hagersville, Haldimand County, Halton Hills, Hamilton, Hanover, Harriston, Hespeler, Ingersoll, Inglewood, Innerkip, Jarvis, Kingston, Kingsville, Kitchener, Lake Superior, Lincoln, Linwood, Listowel, London, Lucknow, Merrickville, Mono, Mount Brydges, Mount Forest, Mount Pleasant, Neustadt, New Hamburg, Newboro, Newport, Niagara-on-the-Lake, Niagara Falls, North Bay, Norwich, Oakville, Onondaga, Orangeville, Orillia, Oshawa, Otterville, Owen Sound, Palmerston, Paris, Parry Sound, Pelham, Perth, Peterborough, Petrolia, Pickering, Port Colborne, Port Elgin, Port Hope, Port Perry, Portland, Preston, Rockwood, Sarnia, Sault Ste. Marie, Seaforth, Sheffield, Shelburne, Simcoe, Smiths Falls, Smithville, Southampton, Southwest Oxford, St. Catharines, St. George, St. Jacobs, St. Marys, St. Thomas, Stoney Creek, Stouffville, Stratford, Strathroy, Sudbury, Tavistock, Terra Cotta, Thamesford, Thunder Bay, Tillsonburg, Toronto, Uxbridge, Waterdown, Waterford, Waterloo, Welland, Wellesley, West Flamborough, Westport, Whitby, Windsor, Wingham, Woodstock, York, Zorra

# Series Name: Cruising Canada
## Saving Our History One Photo at a Time
### in colour photos